Through the Eyes of a Poet The Life and Writings of Kate Fort Codington

Dory Codington

DorysHistoricals Press
2014

Dory's Historicals Press
www.doryshistoricals.com

Published by DorysHistoricals Press Newton, MA
Printed in the United State of America

DorysHistoricals Press
2014

First Edition

Books by Dory Codington: Edge of Empire Series

Cardinal Points
Fate and Fair Winds
Beside Turning Water

Please Visit Dory at http://www.DorysHistoricals.com
Facebook author page at
 http://www.facebook.com/DorysHistoricals

This book is dedicated to my father, John Fort Codington, his children, grandchildren, nieces, nephews, in-laws, cousins and friends.

Contents

Introduction

I began this project in 1979, four years after the death of my grandmother, Kate Fort Codington. My family has a long tradition of writing short biographies and genealogies, so as I was uncertain where my life would go that summer, my father asked me to put together my grandmother's poems and short stories and write a short biography. It was an interesting project and I enjoyed traveling to interview her friends and visit my cousins and aunts. But the material told a story more vast than I expected, so instead of merely putting the poems and stories together, I decided to arrange them into a biographical sketch and write historical essays on her parents' families and influences on her writing.

Although Kate Codington's first published poem appeared in her local newspaper when she was seven, the first ones included here ran in a column in The Macon Daily Telegraph in 1915 and 1916. She wrote short stories in the 1920s and 1930s, and although she wrote poems throughout her life, she collected and published her poems later in 1966 and in 1975, just months before her death. Included in this work are excerpted and slightly altered bits from her unpublished novel, Cypress Knees – specifically where the story is autobiographical.

I finished the editing, compilation and short introductions in 1983, just before Kate Codington's 100th anniversary and one month after the birth of my daughter, Katy. I made copies and handed the work to family members. Of course I was asked whether I was going to try to publish? But I didn't see enough cohesion in the work, and believed that no one but family would be interested in old newspaper columns and poems.

The world has changed in thirty years, now those columns are nearly a century old. Kate Codington's stories about the 1926 hurricane have assumed a new importance as we try to gain some sense of what the weather used to be. Her poems and their essence of joy, have new importance, and now with Atlanta grown beyond anything my grandparents could have imagined, there is a bit of nostalgia for the Atlanta's middle years.

One of the greatest changes in the past thirty years has occurred in the publishing world. As traditional publishers have conglomerated and disappeared, the digital and self-publishing world has bloomed. This has allowed non-traditional works to become available to interested readers. Because of my own writing, a skill in storytelling and drama I attribute to my grandmother and her novelist brother John Fort II, I entered the world of digital book publishing, formatting and re-formatting, and during a recent visit to Atlanta, Georgia, I decided to update and publish this work.

I have changed the order of the chapters, as well as the poems and stories within them. My two history degrees demanded that I put the work in chronological order, rather than the artistic vision I constructed when I was a young music major.

I have re-edited my chapter introductions, but I have not modernized my observations on train travel that I set out in the 1970s, nor have I revisited my memories of my summers with Mamama. So this book will stand as two histories, one that is my own journey into the past, and the other, Kate Fort Codington's journey and observations during her long and wonderful life.

A word on the arrangement of narrative and poems is in order. Most of the historical narrative was written by my aunt, Catherine Codington Shafer, for this work between 1975 and 1981. Her words are labeled, mine are not. William E. Fort, Kate Codington's brother contributed a short reminiscence about Cooleewahee, the Fort family's winter home during the 1886 Christmas, and my father helped me with his memories and letters, which filled in my own throughout the work. Poems and stories without a credited author were written by Kate herself. Her poems, used within the narrative, are labeled with the book title and year of publication. All works are listed in the Notes by title except narratives constructed by her neighbor, Emily Anderson Hightower, my aunt, Catherine Codington Shafer, my father, John Fort Codington, and myself.

Through the Eyes of a Poet
The Life and Writings of Kate Fort Codington

Preface

Southern history fascinates us. Over a century later we continue to make movies and write stories about America's Civil War and the ante-bellum South. We view with delighted horror overseers whipping small black children, and pig-headed Southern ladies going down in glory with their beloved plantations.

We have lost the thread that the war slackened but did not break: of a nation with a common history and joint future.

We don't recognize Northerners who didn't want to fight the South; or Southerners who, for whatever reason, did not believe in secession. We think of the ante-bellum Southern white as rather foolish, and rich, tied to a single tract of land from which neither fire, pillage, nor death could tear him,(or should I say her, since all white men disappear in popular literature by 1863 except on the battlefield and bedroom)

Nowhere in our consciousness do we make room for the Southern professional - a thinker who was the product of a heritage that included doctors, lawyers, and statesmen, or a naturalist who devoted his efforts to agriculture and the study of birdlife, or a physician who treated illness as well as bullet wounds.

Kate Fort Codington was a product of the thinking, professional South. Born in 1883, she was a poet and a writer of prose. Politically astute, she inherited a hatred of war from her father, a lieutenant in the 1st Georgia Regulars, Confederate army. She was an environmentalist, a pacifist, a humanist, a feminist, a believer in equal rights, and the devoted mother of six.

Kate Fort Codington continued writing until her death in 1975. It is her observations of this century that I have tried to portray. Rather than painting the South as a barbaric netherworld with a wash of gentility, I have tried to see the South, and the world, as a whole through the eyes of a sensitive and intelligent Southerner - Kate Fort Codington's, the eyes of a poet.

Portrait Of A Lady

"Come to tea," she said.
  And so I went.
The afternoon was more than tea with lemon
  in dainty cups and cookies she had baked.
She shared her wisdom of the years with
  quiet dignity,
each word a polished gem,
  like her poems.
Her face made softer, framed in white,
    she sat erect on her antique sofa and talked of
      learning ...
(Always she was learning some new thing.)

She spoke
  of helping someone far less agile than she
of love ...
  and there was music in the words she used...
her love for all her children ... their children.
  and even me.
How fortunate I was to drink her tea
  and come away
to feel my youth returned ... a whole new life   to
  live!

Aurelia Austin, 1975

From a Train Window

The dawn is lost where shadows fawn and lift
Their dingy veils from chimney-tops, and bare
Old buildings stumbling drunken down the rift
Of alley-ways; their eyes the empty stare
Of broken glass -encrusted by the grime
Of rain and soot - a lethal interplay,
Puncturing scars of negligence and time
With final dereliction and decay.

The train moves on. New buildings amplify
The sudden brightness. Shafts of sun and blue
Sweep to a weeded park. A car slips by,
While trucks and buses down the avenue
Startle the early silence. From a lawn
A woman waves...
The engine blows his horn.

Shod With Light, 1966

September, 1979. I am on a train heading south to begin this project. There is no doubt that Southern Railway is the best ride going. The trains are old, by Amtrak standards, and more or less unchanged since at least the 1940s. The bathrooms have a lounge with three sinks and the coaches have seats with retractable armrests; something that the air lines invented some thirty years later.

The only change that upset me was the change from starched cotton on the back of each chair to Amtrak's sterile filter paper. The pillows that used to cost fifty cents three years ago were also gone. They'd been replaced with more filter paper stuffed with polyester batting. Those old pillows had cold clean cotton cases outside real goose down with striped ticking. The dining car is unchanged. The food is good, heavy American cooking, but tasty.

The table cloths are starched cotton, and the plates and cups are weighted so they don't move as the train screeches around curves and south. Monday afternoon, I settled into my seat at 2:35, and at 2:55 the train pulled out of Pennsylvania Station, New York and into the bright September sunlight.

I was going south and the only way to find the old south is to bring the south to New York and take Southern Railway into the past. Southern Railway "Serves the South" and "Gives a Green light to Innovation", I read on the sides of freight car trains parked in New England and New York, but this is a train, not a commuter option. On Amtrak, the conductor takes your ticket and exchanges it for a color coded tag which, he says, "you must keep with you at all times."A conductor on Southern Railway writes your destination in his little book so that the porter can wake you and get your baggage to the door in time. Not only does the conductor know you've paid, but the porter and the conductor knows who you are, and where you're going and they care as a matter of professional pride.

The biggest problem with Southern Railway is that Amtrak has cut the scheduled runs from New York to New Orleans to one train daily. So that Atlanta, my destination and the proud possessor of the second largest airport in-the world, has but two passenger trains passing through each day. One of those trains is going from New York to New Orleans and the other travels to New York from New Orleans. When I called Amtrak for the schedule and discovered that there was only one train to Atlanta, I was disappointed. I'd wanted to watch the sunset over the Virginia hills. But it was too late in the summer, and the train didn't pass by there in time for the sunset.

In the dusk south of Washington, I know from memory the leaves are greener and the earth redder. The sunset would have been powerful, the sky to the west shining a ruby gold. We head south, and the landscape becomes thicker, a temperate jungle, so much greener than the sparse New England landscape of my home.

In the moonlight and the street lights of an occasional town, I see that the woods are now covered with kudzu. Kudzu, a Japanese vine, was originally planted by some well meaning agriculturists to prevent erosion on the banks of highways and railroad tracks. It has now covered entire forests and killed almost everything underneath its ghostlike outline.

By Charlottesville the train is two hours late - what's that about the south being slower? They must be referring to the train. Nowadays the south isn't slower, but the south was slower in years past. Slower and prettier, calmer and older. Somewhere, along the line we've acquired a few more conductors and the passengers don't care so much that we're late - they only feel sorry for the folks on the waiting end I'm waiting too, waiting for morning so I can see the beauty of this southern landscape. My memories of Georgia melt into one long summer, of mountains and rivers, green leaves of pine, laurel and rhododendron, of climbing crepe myrtles and listening to choruses of crickets and katydids.

Clemson, South Carolina! I look out the window and see the sign on the low white train station. I wake to large stately trees, red clay and southern houses with spacious lawns. Between the green jungles of kudzu are open fields, some of corn and some green, marked by an occasional cow. Wet clay roads winding between the fields and up the hills, reminds me of my father's stories of his mother driving the six children in her small Model T on steep unpaved mountain roads, the wet clay sending the car skidding while she held the fussy baby in her arms. It sends shivers down my spine.

The mountains get taller and their numbers increase as we head west... toward Atlanta. Through miles and miles of South Carolina, These South Carolina hills are, I will learn, where Kate's mother Lulah Ellis Fort grew up, but now I am anxious for Georgia.

Mt. Airy. A familiar and wanted station sign. We are in northwest Georgia, close to Mountain Hall, the beloved family home of the Forts. Cornelia, I see the big red apple in the middle of town. This huge red monument was designed by my great-aunt Martha, in honor of that important crop her father, John P. Fort, cultivated and grew in these hills.

At 10:30 a.m., only 45 minutes late, the train pulls into Atlanta. "Southern Serves The South."

The State of Georgia lies at the southern end of the Appalachian Mountains, between Alabama and the sea. To her south is Florida, and her coast is luxurious with sea islands and marshes. The land is fertile, and varies from lowlands of the south to the hills of the Piedmont and the high mountains of the Blue Ridge in the far north. The weather varies from hot tropical breezes on the Sea Islands and on the Coastal Plain, to the plain heat and the bitterly cold but blessedly short winters in the interior. But in the mountains, whose rain and snow supply much of the water to a watery state, the weather is similar to that of New England. Wetter and colder than the rest of the state, its winter freezes and hillsides covered with ice and snow lead to spring melts that feed the rich system of rivers that flow through the state. These mountains are also full of ancient underground springs, which bubble to the surface and join the melt. And under the surface of the earth, far below the dark red clay and thick, noxious swamps that cover the southern counties, are a series of rivers known as aquifers, pristine water available to those who had the vision to find it.

The fertile region in the center of the state was still a wild frontier before Kate's birth in 1883. The battles of the American Revolution fought by her great-grandfathers Arthur Fort and Daniel Low, and in the War of 1812 by her grandfather Tomlinson, included Indian, British and Tory opponents, not regular militia. These were frontier battles reminiscent of our vision of the wild west. Kate's grand mother, Martha Fannin Fort, described large rattlesnakes, and untamed land, in her memoir recorded by her daughter Kate Haynes Fort in Memoirs of the Fort and Fannin Families, (Chattanooga, 1903).

The central counties of the state grew in the years immediately after the American Revolution, as settlers from the Georgia's coastal counties and Virginia arrived seeking the rich farmland and pleasant climate of the region. The story that Martha Fort told shows that the family moved between Warren, Hancock, Putnam and Baldwin counties. Georgia has had five capitols, and at the time covered by her memoir it was moved from Louisville northwest to Milledgeville, Baldwin County. The state would move its capitol one more time, to Atlanta, in 1868, proving the early thesis that the state was always moving its people and power north and west.

The Fort family lived in Milledgeville, where Tomlinson was a well respected physician. He is known for his service as a surgeon on the Florida front in the War of 1812; his single term representing

Georgia in the US Congress and seven terms in the Georgia Legislature, and helping to found the Georgia Medical College. Tomlinson studied medicine in Philadelphia in 1808-09. His lasting work is his Treatise on Internal Medicine, published in Milledgeville, in 1849.

John Porter Fort was the ninth of twelve children born to Tomlinson and Martha Fannin Fort. He was born in 1841, and like his two older brothers he enlisted in the Georgia Regulars when Georgia seceded in March, 1861. John had recently finished at Oglethorpe College, and was reading for the law. He served in various regiments in Virginia, Florida and in the interior of Georgia, harassing Sherman's troops from Savannah into South Carolina, and as he put it the flame of patriotism called until the final surrender and arrest of Jefferson Davis.

He returned to civilian life in 1865. After some time spent in the outdoors to heal from an incessant cough, he moved back with his family then living in Macon. He started a law practice with his brother-in-law, and because of deaths in the family, he became estate manager for property owned by his young nieces and nephews being cared for by his mother. He soon bought land of his own in Houston, Lee and Dougherty counties. He continued his law practice until 1885 when he "turned his life completely over to agriculture", as he put it.

Since he was a young child, John had always been fascinated by the natural world. He was a keen observer, what in the nineteenth century was known as a 'naturalist'. He amazed his young siblings that he was able to predict when a parent bird would return to feed its young, timing it to the second. He discovered a parasite to the cotton caterpillar that was decimating the cotton crop and the industry dependent on it. It would be John Fort's agricultural interests, as well as the educational opportunities for his children, that would lead to the family moving between city and country, south Georgia to north.

As a writer and poet, Kate Codington would incorporate her family's journey into her writing. Like her father, she had a deep love of nature, understanding and appreciating each living thing. Each place they lived gave her a deep appreciation for her surroundings and topics for her poetry.

South Georgia

In the winter of 1881 John P. Fort would change the landscape and living conditions in southwest Georgia. In his memoir, dictated to his daughter Martha E. Fort and published in 1918, the year after his death, he wrote:

> *The terrain of southwest Georgia is noted for its extreme beauty and abundance of wildlife. Much of the land in this region was at this time interspersed with swamps. The land is very fertile, but in the summer months fresh water was not to be found. The mosquitoes that bred in the swamps and deep stagnant pools carried malaria and bilious fever.*

> *My reasons for the faith I had in the practicality of artesian wells being bored in Georgia was a matter of thought and observation extending from my boyhood. One day while in a buggy with my father in the lower part of Baldwin County, we crossed a little stream known as Reedy Creek. It flowed over many small round pebbles that looked like birds' eggs. The banks, too, of the stream were covered with these round stones imbedded in the earth. I got out of the buggy to get some as checker rocks for my sisters. My father explained to me, that at an ancient period of time this had been the shore of the ocean that had extended over what is now southern Georgia, south of a line drawn from Augusta to Columbus. I was interested in the facts explained to me by my father, and remembered the conversation.*

> *Many years afterwards while on the Chattahoochee River I noticed, cut by the river bank a stratum of blue earth, which I felt assured was an ocean deposit known as blue marl, a deep sea ooze. This ooze is impervious to water, preventing the water underneath from rising to the*

surface in springs. I noticed this deposit on the west bank, the Alabama side, and that it was sloping downward, eastward and toward the south. I crossed over to the east bank, the Georgia side, none was to be seen. But the natural supposition was that it was only lower than the river bank. This was near Eufala. As this marl appeared again at the surface near Brunswick, I took what seemed to me to be a logical position that this deposit extended under all southern Georgia, far down in the earth.

It was a site on the "Hickory Level Plantation" that I chose for his experiment. We began February 1, 1881, I continued the work through the summer. My tools were so inferior that I almost had to abandon the well, especially when a boring tool, a reamer, was broken off in the in the bottom of the pipe. My well seemed to be a failure and was ridiculed by some of the citizens of Albany. I remember one day on the street that a Mr. Brazemore, a warehouse man, stopped me and laughingly said that he had an injunction against me, because I was trying to rival Noah — the difference was that Noah wished to rescue from a flood while I wanted to flood the State. Such ridicule only made me more than ever determined to go on.

On August 1st, I returned to Macon leaving word to continue work until my return, which would be within a few days. On August 4th, at ten o'clock in the morning I received the following telegram, "Water flowing at seven gallons per minute".

The story of the first artesian well in Georgia would feature in newspapers and history books, it would as well become part of Kate's novel, Cypress Knees written in the 1960s and unpublished.

Silently Brooks led them through the afternoon of shimmering corn stalks to the cotton field. "Here it is. Moses done struck the rock."

Buford ran forward and knelt beside the little pipe. The artesian was flowing, clear and limpid from the earth, down the trough, overflowing and tumbling into the reservoir with the gentle purr of doves. Buford let the water enfold his hands and face, then he drank. "Oh God how wonderful!"

Buford lingered on his knees in a haze of joy and thanksgiving. Yes God was good. Whatever his faith had been, he knew now that this was true. Suddenly he could picture the people coming, in wagons, with buckets, sick and heavy laden. Even his own child, he could see her drink, her eyes alight and sunshine on her hair. Here was health for the people and drink for the small green crops that could be planted. Here on Kioka was fresh water, the greatest gift from the earth, a gift of health.

Of her father, Kate Codington would write –

...Note of thrush
And wild heart of the trees.
There 'mid glooms of cypress brooding moss
And lakes of ebon pearl,
With shy wood denizens and mist of boughs
He met his God.
Day beckoned him, and forth among the fields
He stepped and sowed his spirit.

Sowed that man might east and live and "thank the Lord,
Giver of all good gifts."...

Excerpt: 'In Memory of John Porter Fort, Kate Fort Codington, 1918 in John Porter Fort.

Fort would go on to drain bilious swamps and build reservoirs, based on the same scientific observation. To prevent, or at least slow down the mosquitoes, supplied the reservoirs with small larva eating fish, and erected gourds and birdhouses for the purple-martin, a swallow known for its voracious appetite for mosquitoes.

Later that same year,1881, John married Lulah Ellis. Lulah dictated a few stories to her daughter, Susan Fort Redfern, in 1935. I have excerpted one here.

As was not uncommon among educated Southerners immediately following the [Civil War], Willie opened a school in Aiken in order to support the family. His brothers and sisters were among the pupils at the school. Studies included arithmetic, algebra, geometry, grammar and Latin. When Lulah was sixteen Willie left the school to study law in Atlanta. To support the family she had no choice but to continue the school. On Friday afternoon she walked out of school a student and returned on Monday, the teacher.

In 1870 the family joined Willie in Atlanta. Lulah began teaching in the Atlanta public school system. She left in 1881, to marry. At that time she was in line for the principalship of Girl's High School.

That winter there was a ball given at the DeGive Opera House in Atlanta, as was the custom of the time, most people watched from the audience while those more bold danced on stage. Lulah, sitting in the audience, had gone with a friend and was introduced to John Porter Fort by his sister Fanny. Later that spring took a trip to New Orleans. Coincidentally John Fort was there at the same time; among the ladies present Col. Fort was considered quite a catch. The hostess sat him next to a charming young woman; "No," he said, "there is a little school teacher from Georgia whom I prefer."

Lulah's life was her husband and her children. She roamed the woods and orchards with John, joining him in foxhunting and riding, as well as helping with more serious agricultural work. And, she was the children's first teacher. Doing lessons with them each day, and singing and reading to them at bedtime. Her grandson John Fort Codington, said as I was working on this project, that she was the only teacher, ever able to explain algebra to him.

Of her mother Kate would write:

> She felt the meaning, not the length of years,
> In joy, resurgent as the ageless spring,
> Her quest was a fulfilment; for her faith,
> Seeing beyond the boundaries of time,
> Beheld the triumph of a perfect
> Completed by her gift of motherhood.

Kate Fort Codington in
Tallulah Ellis Fort: A
Memoir

Kate was the second of six children, three girls and then three boys. Her father's law practice was in Macon, where the first children were born. His agricultural interests always in mind, in 1885 John and Lulah decided to spend the winter at "Cooleewahee" a plantation in Dougherty County, he had recently purchased. The Forts loved this area so much they spent many winters at Cooleewahee after that first year, from then on dividing their time between the plantation and their home in Macon.

South Georgia

You pines, forever rimmed against the sky
Blue stalks, gray plumes and arrow cuts of cone,
With limb white-dead, flung naked as a cry
You sway as sea-lights, but you stand as stone.
A-down the earth new forests wake and croon.
Wide leaves spray sun in cooling ministries
To bird, to reef, to highway burnt with noon,
Chapeling their praise in Druid sanctities.

But stark I see you, hushed, eternal pines,
Linked as a chain of brothers round the world,
Spaced to the throb of far horizon lines,
Young with the green of centuries unfurled,
Lifting the dawn above your prison gate,
Reaching to God your arms insatiate.

Shod With Light. 1966.

Kate's brother, William Ellis Fort wrote this reminiscence of their plantation Cooleewahee in a correspondence to John Fort Codington in 1976.

A Reminiscence: Christmas 1886

Our family was living that winter on a plantation owned by my father some nine miles southwest of Albany, Georgia and reached by a main road running to the far reaches of the County and--beyond. The plantation we lived on was called Cooleewahee, after the song of the wood thrush, and to the family, Father, Mother and children it compared most favorably to heaven, in fact it was superior because its delights were now available and there was no waiting to-enjoy them. Just why this plantation was so revered by the family had always been something of a mystery to people who never lived there, Cooleewahee was a fairly large plantation as plantations went in that area. It contained three thousand acres and was practically square, being founded on the north by the County Road, on the east by the "Big Woods," a virgin forest of long leaf pines, on the south by Smut Eye Plantation and on the west by Cooleewahee swamp, a mile through which a creek of the same name lazily wound its way to the Flint River. Ah, this swamp! In it were deer, black bear, raccoons, beaver, mink, otter and countless water moccasins and turtles. On a drive through the swamp on the causeway you could see the turtles and snakes on a warm winters day sunning themselves by the roadway and at the approach of the carriage the turtles would drop in the water with a plop and the snakes would slowly slither away in the long grass. The swamp also was covered with a virgin forest of cypress, ash, magnolia, water oak and other water loving trees and shrubs.

The center of the plantation was given over to farming, corn and especially cotton being the chief crop. The house where we lived was about a half mile distant from the County Road. If you have a mind a plantation mansion of two stories with balconies and tall white columns in front and surrounded by magnolia trees as you see in the movies, you had best forget the picture. Our home was a small cottage of four rooms, a hall in the center, small front and back porches and a semidetached kitchen in the rear. It was in a grove of oak trees and it was painted white, however, it was originally built to be occupied by a white overseer back in slavery times. There were no homes for owners on plantations in this area as all this countryside was owned by absentees. This section of Georgia was considered very sickly except for the four months our family lived there in the cold weather. Malaria was rampant in the summer and white and black alike had a hard time with chills and fever. At present time this is a healthful area year round, as the Malaria bearing anopheles mosquito has been eradicated.

Kate wrote this short story about a pet deer that lived with the family on the Cooleewahee plantation.

The Adventures of Billie

Suddenly we children felt infinitely important—
there was not another family in the whole of our town
that possessed a deer. Yet here he was under Mr.
Cheshire's arm, his long legs dangling, his coat flecked
with white splotches, and his fathomless eyes looking
at us with the mute, startled question of all wild,
swamp born creatures.

"Looks like he's been under the cotton gin,"
someone remarked. But Mr. Cheshire spoke seriously,
stroking the delicate transparent ears, "his mother was
kilt, or I guess it were something like that. I was down
about a mile in the swamp when I seed this little chap
a-looking at me from beside a rotten cypress."

Mr. Cheshire loved children and pets. And when he
drove to town from my father's plantation,- where he
held the position of overseer, there was usually
something beside an armload of sugar cane stored
away in the buggy. But what was a rabbit, a squirrel or
even a baby alligator compared to a real, live baby
deer?

I'm sure that my brothers and sisters felt much of
my enthusiasm. But when timidly I put out my hand
and touched Billie's forehead, I experienced all the
passionate love and possessiveness possible to a
healthy little girl of nine years. Secretly in my heart, I
knew that Billie belonged to me.

Looking back to our experience with Billie, I
believe that it was our parents who were the real young
at heart. Without demur Billie was accepted into the
household of six children— three dogs and cats
instantly assuming roles of minor importance. Billie
was given a bottle of milk and taught to sleep on a

white wooly rug beside by Mother's bed. Soon he was lapping Baby Jimmy's prepared food from a saucer, then, as his legs grew strong and long, he would scamper to the dining room to drink his coffee from a thin china cup on the hearth. How we children adored him, giggling with glee and pride as he drank the bright warm liquid which lay so many years beyond our own childhood experience.

But time runs quickly with animals. Before we knew it he was sleeping in a big wooden box under the back porch, leaping around the fountain in the front yard, mangling the violets and jonnie-jump-ups beneath his dancing, happy little hoofs. On the evening when my Mother and Father entertained the euchre club, it was an accepted fact that Billie would be among those present. Mr. Cheshire had brought in a buggy load of yellow jessamine from the swamp with which to decorate the house for the card party. So with her usual artistry, Mother tied a great bow of yellow ribbon around the neck of the all too willing deer.

Never expecting to sit up for a grown up party, and utterly without jealousy, we children filed away to bed. But we roared with delight the next morning at the tales of how Billie with perfect composure had ambled among the guests, visiting each in turn each of the ten card tables, and always allowing the ladies to play with his ears.

It was not long after this that the family planned an all day outing on the plantation. While only ten miles distant, it required about two hours for the horses to pull the carriage through the sand-beds and rain-puddles of the old fashioned road. We started soon after breakfast. Billie was left in the house, and the servants were instructed not to turn him out until an hour after our departure.

Billie however, knew the test of freedom. With one leap he plunged through the frosted glass of the front door and without a scratch on his young body was up with the carriage before we reached the corner. All the way to the plantation he ran beside us, sometimes darting ahead or skimming with unmitigated joy across an adjacent cotton field. Sometimes we children were terrified, thinking him lost. Always he would return, buoyant and unafraid, trusting on the sure speed of his long and beautiful legs. Right here I must say that there was an unusual philosophy in our family. We praised Billie for his amazing feat; I don't remember that our Father scolded him for the broken door, which certainly must have cost something to replace.

As Billie developed, so did his appetite. In many respects he was an epicure, especially regarding peanuts— ground peas we called them in South Georgia. His sensitive lips were annoyed by the rough shells. And because we children respected his whims, he became intolerant. One day, smelling ground peas in my pocket, he cornered me in the hall and began nuzzling and pressing against me in his eagerness. Shelling ground peas is a slow job and Billie became furious at the delay. Suddenly he leaped upon me with his front feet and began tearing my apron to shreds. My screams brought the rest of the family, and Billie was spanked and sent to the backyard. But I wept on, not so much from the physical pain as from spiritual hurt. I knew that our old playfellow days were over forever. Billie had betrayed my love and I was afraid of him.

"See his horns," Father remarked, touching the stubs on top of Billie's head, "he will soon be dangerous."

One morning Vickie our nurse, informed us that

every night now, when we, thought Billie was asleep under the back porch, he was on the far side of town, running up and down the banks of Flint River, and followed by a train of dogs. She laughed at our frozen horror.

"Don' you bother," she said, "them dogs ain't pesterin' Billie. They's playin'.They's havin' fun."

This was wonderful. Terror gave way to admiration. Vickie was right--no dog could catch him. As for me, how I would have loved to run with him in the misty moonlight, shouting, laughing, playing tag down the banks of the dark forbidden river.

Billie's last days were most amazing. No longer were there barriers to his freedom. Light as a swan he would soar at will over the iron picket fence which enclosed our front yard, his whole body steering for the river. On, on he would run without a backward look, knowing that a rabble of yelping dogs would follow in his wake. Never was there such a hero, never such insane and joyous play. He was known all over our little city of Albany. Everybody grinned, everybody was amused.

Always we were greeted by such remarks as "I saw Billie here." "I saw Billie there."

If our pet had lived in this generation, I would have compared his leaps and races to the flights of a plane, a plane which for no visible reason landed one day in flames.

The iron pickets of our fence for months had been a bagatelle to Billie. These were the first hurdle in the glorious exploit of day. But early one morning, just at sunrise, he was too eager, too hurried. As he was impatient for his ground peas, now he was impatient for the river, or was it for his heritage of the swamp lying beyond, or the unknown mate awaiting him. His mind clear, his feet were suddenly confused. Quickly, hopelessly he fell upon the long relentless spikes.

Father was accustomed to rise early and dress before the rest of us were up. This morning through the open door I saw him enter Mother's room and leaning over whisper something in her ear. Then I heard her sobbing, and I knew, even before I was told, then the bright adventure of Billie was over forever.

I have taken a short story Kate wrote of a fictional girl and edited it, but it was her own experience she wrote of, and one she vividly remembered.

To Kate at the age of six, the pile of cotton was a pile of snow, offering excitement. Only once had she seen real snow, then only for a half an hour and it had appeared like a swarm of white butterflies among the roses. She and her brothers and sisters had shouted and played in it.

"Some day, Brooks," she had said, watching the pyramid trickle away into water, "I'm going to jump into the ginhouse cotton and play like it's snow."

Brooks had turned on her fiercely. "Kate, don't you dare. The dust'll choke you clean to death! Lord, half the sand in the field is in that cotton."

Now, unobserved in the dark room, Kate's eyes glowed with excitement. She remembered Brooks' warning but then Brooks had been trying to fool her and keep her from mussing up the cotton. Dusty? Why jumping in that pile would be like jumping in a cloud. Kate's emotions sometimes carried her to great heights. When that happened her face blanched, her lips tightened and she leaped, physically and spiritually, regardless of the consequences. Now she sprang into the pyramid of cotton. The horror was instant. A headlong plunge into a tar barrel could hardly have been more terrible. Her eyes, nose and throat were clamped shut by the flying dust. Through her agony, she heard screams in the back of her head and felt her feet convulse.

She came to with her mother leaning over her and bathing her face with a towel. "God saved you from your own rashness," she said gently.

Opening her eyes, Kate saw the moss tree drooping her silver feathers above her and not far away the glimmering white of Cooleewahee. Then Brooks spoke and his voice was like sobbing.

"How come I looked back, Miss Lulah, only the lord knows. I smelt the dust and saw the cotton-pile-a'settin' crooked."

It was clear from her long life, that not only did Kate have people who loved her to protect her from her foolishness, but in time she learned sense.

Catherine Shafer, her second child, wrote of her mother in an essay for this project, that Kate's sense of adventure and exuberance for life touched every thing she did and wrote. As a young girl she was a "tomboy" with physical strength that was unusual in a girl of the 1880's.

She could do twelve "Giant Swings," something now done on parallel bars in gymnastics. Kate did these swings, until an older woman, much the product of her own generation, told her that while she was upside down her dress came over her head and anyone watching could see her bloomers.

The comment curtailed Kate's swinging upside down, but nothing could contain her sense of adventure. This would last throughout her life which she considered to be a joyous adventure.

Catherine Shafer, Personal Correspondence, 1979.

North Georgia:

In 1886, John Fort decided to give up his law practice and work in agriculture full time. He and Lulah had fallen in love with the mountains near their vacation spot in Rabun Gap. So that year, the family went north for their first summer, in north Georgia. It was then they began to divide their time between Macon and the mountains.

"We bought a small cottage in Mount Airy, Habersham County," which was named Sunshine Cottage."

Georgia Moutains

These mountains are but clouds made permanent,
Preserving luster, curve and undulation
Rich in earth. Their transmutation
Made possible by trees, whose green event
(Like broidered curtain or a pleasure tent)
Covers, contains, and folds in close relation
Peek and cliff - a wild configuration
Of bare design and tangled ornament.

Each geometric pattern of the skies
Repeats itself in verdure. Under trees
Frail petals reach and radiate from heaven
That whirls a nebula. And man is wise,
Whose faith derived from beauty that he sees,
Finds heaven in earth, and earth in all of heaven.

April Thoughts, 1966

In 1898, Susan and Kate started at Piedmont College in nearby Demorest, a small town not far from their home in Mt. Airy, the family moved there for the school year. That same year the Forts bought "The Lanier Place," from a cousin of the famous poet. A beautiful house, built originally as a convalescent home, it sat on the highest point in Mt. Airy. It had wonderful views and wide halls, the children renamed the house "Mountain Hall."

Mountain Hall sits high on the hill above "Sunshine Cottage", the Forts' first home in the small town. The drive from the road to the house is more over-grown now than eighty-two years ago, but it's beauty is undeniable. Just down the drive from the house is a brick well, with 'FORT' clearly carved in the middle of its bricks.

The house sits square behind a circular drive with a chestnut oak in the center, and the first thing I notice, that I have always noticed, about Mountain Hall are the porches. The top floor has a sleeping porch that runs the entire width of the house. Over it is an old tin roof, black with dirt and algae. In the center is a fenced in observatory, located to watch the sunsets over Yonah.

It is, however, the downstairs porch that is the most impressive feature at the front. Covered with trumpet vines and wisteria, it is wide enough to fit a porch swing and breakfast table, and still allow room for children to use it as a covered track. The porch made a continuous loop around the house: one lap:1/2mile, measured by my father who, as he's often said, was born running. In the 1960s the porch was blocked off to enlarge and winterize the kitchen by enclosing it within the main house.

A trestle of vines shade the porch and keep the side and back cool even on the hottest days. Humming birds fly in and out of these colorful flowers, occasionally mistaking a pretty dress for blossoms, or hair for bits of twig - something that was attested to regularly by Martha Anderson, Kate's younger sister, who lived in the house until the 1970s, and was often mistaken for nesting material by the resident hummingbirds.

The interiors of both floors are marked by the two halls that gave the house its name. They extend from front to back on both floors, the rooms branching off from the sides. Downstairs, where now there are faded magazines, dusty books, old furniture and taxidermied specimens, were once sitting rooms, a library and a formal dining room. The second floor has nine bedrooms, the front open to the sleeping porch. All of these rooms were used in the summers, years later, when the offspring of Lulah and John's six children all came to visit at once.

When the Fort children were young, what surrounds the house now as overgrown meadow and forest was a tennis court, a cow pasture, and a cultivated rose and vegetable gardens. Far down the hill behind the house, in the area now bordering the Chattahoochee National Forest and covered in kudzu, was one of John Fort's three peach orchards. His other commercial orchards were in towns further north.

Even with the overgrowth of tall trees, the view from Mountain Hall is spectacular. The windows and small clearings give hints of what it must have been like when John and Lulah were alive, when the front was kept clear so the mountains were visible from the porch.

Sitting there, in the cool breezes of a North Georgia evening, the Forts watched the sun set, "just to the left of Mt. Yonah," the closest, and most majestic of the dozens of mountains visible from Mt. Airy to the south, among small gentle hills. The range of high mountains begins some twenty north-west of Mt. Airy, and almost due north from the house is Tallulah Ridge. This spot was particularly attractive to the Fort children, who loved to go for day trips to the Tallulah Falls and Gorge, near the Tallulah Ridge.

One summer up at Mt. Airy, Kate and her sister Martha decided to visit a friend. To get there they had to take the little wood powered train that ran through the mountains. The girls were already at the station when they realized that they'd forgotten their train fare. They told their story to the ticket man, who talked to the conductor, who talked to the engineer, who talked to the fireman. The fireman told the girls that they could ride for free if they rode on the wood pile. To reach their destination the little train had to go over Tallulah Gorge, a high canyon with a raging river about 1000 feet high.

Kate and Martha climbed on the wood-pile and could feel themselves drop every time the fireman drew out another piece of wood. They made the trip safely, enjoyed their day, and instead of braving the woodpile again, borrowed money for the return trip.

Kate told the story to her children, and her grandchildren relishing the retelling and adding great drama as the girls dropped each time the wood was

taken for the fire. From the glee with which she
recounted that day it was clear she'd loved the
adventure.

Catherine Shafer, Personal Correspondence, 1979

Toccoa Falls

One must gaze long on a waterfall
ere it become
motionless
a picture on a rock
plunge and spark
and windy blue
the stroke of an artist brush.

And one must listen, listen
ere the roar
and foamy diapason
mute to the cool abstraction
of the brain.

Sound and movement interlock
to form the silences.
A rainbow flies the cataract
yet both are still.

Ark of the Everglades, 1975

The mountains of North Georgia seem to hang still in a world of misty waterfalls fed by underground streams. Seventy foot tall trees and rhododendron hug the mountain sides and send their roots over and through the rocky hillsides to anchor in the mossy soil. The blue haze which gives the region its name, holds moisture close to the earth, and the enormous rainfall and high humidity keep the undergrowth thick and green. Butterflies and birds fill the air.

Further north, deeper into the tall mountains, the soil loses its redish tint as the decaying undergrowth turns into rich black topsoil held onto the mountains by the gnarled stems of mountain laurel and azalea that bloom in the spring with white and pink blossoms. Toward summer the Flame Azaleas break up the pastel landscape with their bright orange flowers. These were the hills of the Cherokee and Chickasaw. These proud people live on in place names and stories linked forever to the mountains and valleys.

In 1916 Kate was commissioned to write a libretto for a cantata based on the legend of Nacoochee. The music was composed by James Robert Gillette, and the work was published by J. Fischer and Brothers, New York. Here is the legend and Kate's libretto.

A Folk Legend of the Cherokee

Before the days of the white man these mountains were the home of the Cherokee. They were a proud and intelligent people whose only vice was their sense of superiority; and they often quarreled with neighboring tribes.

During a lull in the disagreement the Chickasaws requested permission to pass through Cherokee land.

Permission was granted if the Chickasaws would stay on the Unicoi trail and stop only at designated spots. One day on their journey a group of Cherokee began taunting the Chickasaws hoping to incite an overt act. The Chickasaws were too clever and nothing happened. However, during the incident a young man, Sautee, stood aloof from the others watching Nacoochee, a beautiful young woman, daughter of the Cherokee Chief. Realizing that Sautee was the son of the Chief of the Chickasaws, they knew that their newfound love would never be sanctioned.

Staying for three days and nights on Mt. Yonah in a cave known only to Nacoochee, they were blissfully happy but knew that soon they must return and convince their fathers to cease their quarreling and reach an agreement.

When they returned Nacoochee's father, Chief Wahoe, was so angry that his beloved daughter would choose a Chickasaw, that he ordered Prince Sautee thrown from the cliffs of Mt. Yonah. As Nacoochee watched from the place where they had been so happy she realized that without Sautee life would hold no promise. She hurled herself after him to the foot of Mt. Yonah. And there at the base of this beautiful mountain Sautee and Nacoochee dragged their broken bodies together, and, locked in this embrace they died.

Seeing their children thus, the warring Chiefs vowed eternal peace and had the two lovers buried together at the junction of two lovely valleys. And so that this sad tale will never be forgotten Wahoe renamed the two valleys Sautee and Nacoochee.

FINALE OF: A LEGEND OF NACOOCHEE
(A cantata of the Cherokees)

Sautee:
With arm and with heart from the wild blue north
    I come, great Currahee,
To bind my tribe to the shaft of your tribe in
    flint-fast unity.
The love of your daughter, her life I seek,
To carry away with me
Over the river that chants and flows on to great
    eternity.

Currahee:
Fulfilled the promise the gods have writ
Deep-cut on the iron hickory trees;
Through marriage with war-sown northern tribe,
Like fire shall sweep the Cherokees.
Nacoochee, come, nor fate delay
The Red Winged hawk Would catch his prey.

Semi Chorus:
The corn bloom sways as the Maid appears,
Fair as the beams that creep
Through wreaths that circle the mountain top,
Where dew-gemmed berries sleep.

Sautee:
Where the dusk lies dim in the canyon deep,
I worship, I worshiped thee;
The light of thy smile through the fogs of the
    steep crept down, crept down to   me;
On dizzying summit I felt the flame of thy spirit,

thy spirit climb,
And rending the veil of the distance,
I clasped and knew thee mine.

Nacoochee:
Mine eyes awake as wild rose to the sun,
My sadness swoons,
My life to tripping summer showers
Thy voice a-tunes.
I see but thee,
I turn to thee, with raptured homing start,
Like the wild grey dove that seeks a rest
From the beatings of her heart.

Sautee:
Star of Eve, the Twilight's silver tear,
Guide of my steps where glades of precipice rear,
Winged with the dazzling dream that the gods let
        fly,
I shatter the gloom to claim thee
Or to die.
Then thou wilt come,
Oh, Radiant One

Nacoochee:
And be thy bride.
O'er clambering ways
Of violet haze.

Sautee:
We will abide.
Star of the Evening,
Shedding joy

Nacoochee:
About thy way:

Sautee:
A herald of the day.

Nacoochee and Sautee:
Love is like the rhododendron bloom
Of crystal white,
A-pink with rosy quartz of morning light.
Love is like the jeweled passion flower
Of amethyst,
The tint of twilight hills above the mist.

Chorus:
Great Spirit, who doth cover they face
With lightning and flood;
Who shooteth the night with arrows of sun
To clouds of blood;
Who bind-eth the year with
Winter's granite bars;
Who wrappeth the year with silence and with
        stars
Unite this twain in ever burning love,
As Yonah melts in light to-day above.

J. Fischer and Brothers, New York, 1916

In 1906, John Fort purchased property near Rabun Gap in Mountain City. The land was not far from the headwaters of the Tennessee River. Research had shown him that the rainfall in this Gap was extraordinarily high. There was an old apple orchard there. Fort planted new ones, hopeful that the climate would produce great apples. Tender care to these old trees resulted in an unblemished, delicious apple. He sent baskets of them to Spokane, Washington. The first year the apple, now named "Fort's Prize," won second place for Southern Apples. The next year, the crop looked even better. In 1909, Fort's Prize was awarded first prize, and it was listed in the pomological books as a new variety.

The people of the mountains interested Kate. She wrote that the Fort girls were not encouraged to play with the local children, but the city girls frightened her. When she finished school, she taught at the small school in Mount Airy, as her mother had.

Children of the Blue Ridge
(A narrative of the American Caste)

Forty years may seem a long time in a person's life, but they amount to little through the coves and among the foothills of the Southern Blue Ridge mountains, where earth lifts her prayer-clenched hands against the sky, unclasping her fingers within the cool beatitudes of mist.

Here the little corn patches come and go - this year smaller, the next larger. Smaller, perhaps from lack of rain, or because the family is "down with typhoid," or because the "government" raided the still and "Pap" is sent to jail. Larger, because one of the "Lowlanders has wanted to try his luck;"but finding that "thar ain't no money much in corn," has started an apple orchard down toward the railroad. This spring a baby is born in the one-room cabin, and perhaps by August another of the little tow-heads is carried across the door-sill to Happy Hollow Grave Yard. "Pretty good luck with her

chi-lun S'mantha alius had - twelve in all - six livin'
and six dead."

But the mountains have cared little for all of this
during these forty years. People are the step children of
the mountains - they must be treated harshly and be
made to pay. It is only the laurel that counts, the
hickory, the poplar, and the pine. And as Isaac of old -
being the real heir - they must inherit the land. But to
show the mother heart for tender life, the mountains
have decreed that in the spring pale arbutus must nestle
among giant roots, and azaleas rainbow the green
steeps. While in autumn, goldenrod and sumac must
flash their wild fire through the bare places. The
strength and inexorable beauty of the seasons - can the
will of man withstand the onslaught?

I belonged to the "Lowlanders," to the aristocracy of
the Old South whose families had known service and
leisure. When I was quite small, my parents bought a
summer home (Sunshine Cottage) in Airy. This tiny
hamlet was cast just where the Blue Ridge mountains
break into the long ridges which stretch, like tentacles
of a sleeping dragon, toward the flat lands of Georgia.
The railroad flashed burnished steel between the crude
pine houses, bringing to the inmates the excitement
and discontent of new contracts.

Each April, our family would leave the cotton
plantation, with its possible malaria, and come to the
mountains. "Airy, Airy - all out for Airy." I can see the
blue-coated porter shambling through the open door,
and feel the thin pungent air against my cheek. Then
the scramble to get out suitcases, lunch baskets, bird
cages, and always a basket of kittens and a pointer dog.
while serene, above the confusion, gleamed the black
faces of Mammy Lou and Juddy, the under nurse.

Arriving at the cottage, the first act of us children was to shed our shoes and stockings, then, to keep from "ketchin 'a death o' cold," dip our feet in the icy water drawn from the hundred foot well. Oh the fun of tiptoeing down the hill, and the squeals of merriment as the sharp igneous pebbles pricked our toes. But after a few days, what interested us most were the native children, who lived along the track or at the isolated corners of the corn fields. The parents of these children had come from the upper mountains, lured by the prospect of prosperity which a railroad invokes. Here they pursued their meager agriculture, worked on the track, or drove hacks for the big summer hotel, which spread the skirts of her wide porches through the shady center of Airy. We were taught never to play with these children - they were dirty, therefore "common." We must wait for our companions until the summer people should arrive, filling the hotel and hilltop cottages, bringing with them servants, horses and carriages.

What idleness possessed the well-to-do in the early nineties! The passion for speed, brought on by the automobile, had not yet arrived. And so the women in their tight corsets, with four or five trunks of frilly dresses and plumed hats, would flock to the mountains and the seashore. Hammocks were popular and euchre the favorite sport. From ten in the morning until midnight pretty "ladies" and well groomed bachelors would be seen about the card-tables, always a box of expensive candies between them. Croquet or a walk to the sulphur spring was considered sufficient exercise for good health.

I felt constrained before the taboo of the mountaineer, but the timidity experienced before these summer visitors was actual pain. The winters of my life had been spent on a wide plantation, with its "big white house" surrounded by the Negro quarters. Naturally then, these stylish, self assured individuals filled me with panic. But I was taught that these people were of my class; and that at regular intervals my little sisters and I must be prepared to call on the city children. How glad I was to get home, take off my shoes and stockings, and climb an apple tree.

My father believed that this region was suitable for grape culture. Years before, a few Swiss immigrants had settled in the green valleys about us. Superior in education to our Nordic mountaineers, and dreaming of their native land, they had planted their yards with grape vines. These little vineyards were kept immaculate and in due season the grapes were pressed into wine. In spite of the laws of a "dry state," this wine was sold and drunk on the premises to the secret delight of the countryside. What did prohibition mean in an isolated country in those days? One of the fascinating terrors of our childhood was to find a "dead drunk" stretched out by the roadside. Ye,t in this strangely mixed community, nothing disgraceful ever seemed to happen.

There was a market in the cities for grapes. So, wishing to develop the region and to supplement his income, my father pressed the lethargic mountaineers into service. Rocks and stumps were pulled from the jagged hillsides, and a real industry began. Now money jingled in the gray jeans of the sweaty men - something better to take to the store than the old time butter and beans, used as barter. The population increased, and a few more rough pine cottages were built about Airy.

To show himself the real possessor of his castle,

each home-builder chopped down every tree in the vicinity of his house, exposing the unpainted boards to the merciless glare of the sun. After he had finished this work of devastation, the woman of the family invariably expressed her idea of beauty by filling tomato cans with geranium slips and huddling them in a confused manner about the doorstep.

A few years passed, and blue and amber grapes hung in the vineyards. The summer visitors suddenly became ingratiating, even to me. With the slightest invitation, they would pass the sulphur spring and accompany us to where the Niagara bunches, often a pound in weight, hung netted from the bees. The mountains looked on smilingly but mockingly. After all, these ridges and foot hills belonged to them.

Our family decided to spend a winter in Airy. The summer people left and cold weather set in. We saw a new spirit of comradery expand in the village. Unkempt men would collect around the red-hot stove at the back of Pickett's store. Here they whittled their sticks, spit their tobacco, and guffawed their jokes. It was easy to relax; there were no white collars about, no fine horse to embarrass the skinny mules and wide-horned oxen hitched to the lamp post. "We don't never wash our team till come spring," blurted Sally Hunt's Jim, puffing up his chest with pride. "What's the use when it spatters hisself all over again."

Then it was that Miss Lake decided to teach me German. She was the daughter of an Episcopal clergyman who had given his life to the cause of a few scattered missions."You won't mind if I teach Kitty Reemy with your girls?" Miss Lake smiled at my mother. "She is a nice, clean child, and her mother is bringing her up above her class. We let her read our books." The next day I went to school with Kitty.

Some years before this "ole Man Reemy" with his wife and baby had come down from Passover. Passover was the last stand of the mountains before they curled their impressionable backs against the sky. "Thar's mo' chance down in Airy," mused ole John. "I kin open up a store and Kitty darlin' kin git her education." He opened up his store, and what a conglomeration it was - bacon, stale cakes, and sleazy yard goods in an indiscriminate pile. Somehow everything in old John's store seemed moth eaten, including old John himself with his protruding eyebrows and dirty shirt. Everybody knew that he sold whisky, but they gave him a certain respect because of his love for "Kitty Darlin'".

Always dressed in quaint ruffles, little Kitty would trip to the store, and from behind the counter sell her father's tawdry goods. Her black curls would be pressed tight about her high ethereal forehead, and her wide gray-blue eyes, shining with an inner complacency, challenged the world its patronage. Her English developed from an early devotion to books and from access to Miss Lake's library, was perfect though stilted. With a gesture, Kitty shed the crudeness of the mountains. and attained the regality of some far-off ancestor, different in color and in culture from the ancestors of the high-voiced, flaxen haired children who played about her. But as time went on, in spite of Kitty's superior beauty and intellect, old John's dirty shirt and whispers of the life in Passover stood as a wall of adamant between her and the summer girls.

I was glad to go to school with Kitty. The fleeting conquests of the summer were past, and the bare hills gave me great loneliness. I had always admired her and been drawn by the faint suggestion of mystery, or was it tragedy, that lingered about her slender shoulders. I did not realize that the ruthlessness of the mountains and the snobbishness of my class had already thrown their shadow upon her. In Miss Lake's school I learned that Kitty loved me. What shy little ministrations she wove about me, gifts so subtle that I was never really able to thank her.

The next summer black rot broke out in the vineyards.

My father, alert and scientifically progressive, did what he could. The vineyards were made blue with spray and the mountain boys, in their patched overalls, were hired to pick off the infected fruit. Nothing helped. The lovely grapes looked as though they had been burned by the foxes of Samson. And so, to keep the evil from spreading, the vines were cut down and the hills deserted. Quietly the roots of the laurel and the pine began to work their way through the soil. The mountains had claimed their own.

But my father refused to acknowledge this cycle.

Again the hills were blasted and peach trees were set out. Three years later, great peaches blushed orange and red from the branches of the new trees. The Georgia peaches, so long favorites, come to their perfection when their roots feed deep into the red clay of the steep hills. The quick success of this venture was heralded over the entire country. A different type of settlers built their homes along the ridges - moneyed men from New York, Canada and California, each eager to create for himself a new experience through the life of his orchard. "We are doing much for the mountain people," said the wife of one of the rich

peach men. "I have asked the store to keep Sapolio."
The call of the peaches went far beyond Passover -
men were needed to pick, nail crates and drive teams.
Women were wanted to grade and pack the fruit.
Covered wagons and open carts, full of eager
mountaineers, came winding down the mountains. The
girls made new ginghams for themselves and the young
fellows took extra scrubbings. Blue-eyed babies were
brought at dawn to the packing houses and laid in
baskets, each given a peach to suck regardless of its
age. Should one of the youngsters fret, its mother, like
a true primitive or ultra modern, would wipe her hands
on her petticoat, unbutton her blouse and give the
kiddie his due.

By this time I had grown up and was leading the
social life prescribed for a Southern girl of the upper
class. Our winters were now passed in the city, and our
cottage in Airy exchanged for a big house on the
highest hilltop. That I should be popular was the
ambition of my many aunts. We were not rich, but
lived well. Our credit seemed boundless. My father had
only to walk into a bank and tell the officials of his
orchards and plantations. They recognized in him the
scrupulous honor that could sacrifice acres with a
smile. Today, our bankers are more concerned with
appraising bonds and pocket books than personalities.

Having lost my old self-consciousness, I enjoyed the
merry summer group; house parties and dances
absorbed the days. Every now and then a gallant beau,
like a regular Lochinvar, would come by the way of the
blazing track. Sometimes when vague longings would
come, and I felt that a part of life was passing me by, I
would slip off and write a poem or walk to the Baptist
meeting house down by the creek, and listen to the

preacher in nasal tones line out the hymns.

And Kitty - she too, had been to college, and once more flitted back and forth to the store where old John still ruled in his soiled shirt. My heart bled for her when our gay crowd would run in looking for cheesecloth for a costume party.

But in her eyes there was still a smile on her lips as old John's "Kitty darlin's" vibrated about the building. With no explanation, Kitty had left the Baptist Church for the little Episcopal Chapel at the foot of our hill. She was given the position of organist. What a quaint, formal picture she made sitting at the little brown instrument with her dark curls and ruffled dress. When services were over, she always pulled black mittens over her rather bony hands. I would stop to speak to her, then embarrassed hurry on to the crowd waiting to escort me up the hill. Kitty would smile, wish me well, but never by the flicker of an eyelash tell me that she cared.

Then I married. There was a house party and many invitations. I invited Kitty, glad that the opportunity had come at last.She wrote me a letter. "Once," she said, "You were a clock to cheer to the whole world. Now you are a watch to give joy to your mate."

That was the summer of the big fruit crop. Refrigerated cars blocked the sidings. Markets were glutted, and the Fruit Exchange seemed powerless. The summer girls flitted about uneasily. Some donned big hats and attempted to pack peaches. But before the paid earnestness of the mountain girls, their efforts were futile. Suddenly there was a new interest to relieve the boredom - a young man of a prominent Atlanta family had been made cashier to the bank. The girls preened themselves and began to plan bridge parties. Soon it was discovered that the object of their activities, Hal Broden, was boarding with Old John Reemy and that he had taken Kitty to church. That was enough. He was dropped like the proverbial "hot cake".

After my wedding, I went away to my new home in Macon determined to put enthusiasm into new pleasures and new responsibilities. Months later, a letter came telling me that Hal Broden had left the bank and that Kitty had a baby. I was shocked, as we all were shocked at such things then. The bitterness which this event evoked in Airy is hard to realize. The natives who had been jealous of Kitty's superiority were intolerant, with the ruthless hate of the mountains. The summer visitors were amused. "What could one expect of the daughter of old John?" "Keep away girls". "Go to see her baby? No". Quiet and stately, Kitty walked the streets, a scorned Hester of "Scarlet Letter".

Again the clouds blackened. Old John was dead, and Kitty was keeping men in her house, city men who would come and stay behind the closed darkness of her blinds.

Another year passed and I returned to Airy, happy with my own baby and yearning for the freshness of the breezes. Kitty lay dying with cancer and wanted to see me. I shall never forget the picture - the big, shaded room with its few pieces of old furniture, the great bed, the white spread, the clean patchwork quilt, the heavy pillows - and Kitty. Her long black hair fell in braids on each side of her perfect forehead, and her eyes shone like those of a seraph. I would have taken the slender hand in mine and kissed it and told her I was sorry. But as always her formal words fell between us.

"I will be quite well soon," she said, "Baby Kitty will need a mother in her education. But first we must have a vacation in the blue mountains"; then almost dreamily, "did the mountains ever call you till they gave you strength to come"? But the call of death was answered first. Sobbing the old mother asked that I play the organ at the funeral. Kitty was to be buried in white satin, a diamond ring on her finger.

It was a rainy day but the little Episcopal church was crowded - belated summer guests, mountain people from miles back, all silent, curious and abashed. After it was over, through tears, I wrote:

> In bridal dress, with flowers bedecked,
> My trophies by my side,
> 0 you who scoffed behold me now
> As into your church I ride.
> The sides of my coach shine waxen as pearl
> My steeds are the men of your pride;
> And I scatter their shams with the whip of my
>   scorn,
> With the scourge of the Christ you denied.
> The robe of the priest floats white as a cloud,
> His voice as a rhyming tide,
> The cross swings, a lantern of sun and of rose,
> The arms of the chancel are wide.
> You cringe in your pews for I enter a corpse
> When into your church I ride.

Then they took Kitty up into the mountains, back to Passover, as they had taken old John. Beneath the laurel, perhaps, these two understanding each other, find rest.

Peaches in North Georgia were not a lasting

success. Late spring freezes, the curculio, the coddling moth, the borer, each wrecked its vengeance. Labor and spraying materials' costs were high, and the hills difficult to fertilize. One by one the peach growers returned to their former homes. Wide orchards were deserted, and goldenrod and blackjack sprouts began again to weave their roots about the blighted peach trees.

But something new had happened. Beneath the herculean strength, thousands of acres have been laid bare; hillsides, ridges, and valleys have been tamed by the energy of the apple planter. Shiny cars run lightly over newly paved roads. The old black bonnet of the mountain woman has been changed to the "store hat", and the dresses of the girls are ordered from Sears-Roebuck. Timber has been cut back, and only in the gorges about Mt. Airy does the laurel dare to bloom. But Georgia apples are not bringing the prices they should, and the new investors are losing money. Will man last, or must he try again? And the children of the Blue Ridge, those who are gradually breaking the bonds of tradition, and finding their way through agricultural and mechanical schools, will they return to share their knowledge with the laurel, the hickory and the pine? Or was their early discipline so hard that they will gladly turn the wheel of the revolving cycle over to the hands of the new experimenters?

Blue Ridge Mountain Pictures

THE PEAKS
Earth lifts her prayer-clenched hands against the
    sky
Unclasping her fingers
Within the cool beautitudes of mist.

AFTER THE STORM
Cloud Birds have caught their wings In the jagged
    blue net of the mountains,
And weary with beating their pinions to rain,
Lie breathless and still.

THE CLIFF
Sheer from the valley, Gnarled, Rock boned,
Thundering back the flame of the tempest,
Yet hiding Within the palms of his crevices
Shy wind-born flowers of the wilderness.

THE CATARACTWhite tears of the dawn,
    Gushing in light,Trickling
    necklace of pearls From the thin grey, of the
    gorge.

Unpublished, no date

Mother had an inborn pride– noblisse oblige might be a better term – that made it as impossible for her to display malaise or frayed nerves as it would be to appear unclothed in public. "The calm Kate," one of my uncles called her. But he was a novelist who delighted in outbursts of temperament, and he did not understand her in the least.

There was no wasted motion at all to be found in Mother, no spinning of wheels, no grinding of gears. She was deeply concerned about many things, but she translated these concerns into swift, purposeful action or dismissed them altogether. If she felt grief – and no one ever felt it more keenly – she accepted this feeling as a part of life, but she never allowed it to get of of proportion or to wash over her again and again. Nor did she indulge in self-recrimination of self-pity. She seemed to recognize all the blind alleys of the spirit and instinctively avoid them.

Kate Fort and each of her sisters taught in the small school in Mt. Airy. One particular event stuck with her. The boys, all larger than she, brought their knives to school. She quickly thought of a creative way to get through the year. Turning a situation around and making a good thing out of a potentially bad or even terrible event was one of Kate's talents...

Catherine Shafer, Personal Correspondence, 1979

The Other David

David stumbled down the clay sidewalk of the village, his eyes glued to the letter in his hand.

He had just been to the Post Office, and Olga Remple, the girl Postmistress, had smiled on him with her quiet brown eyes. Old Jim, Olga's father, half tipsy but good humored, had smiled too. People of small communities sense joy or grief in one another... There was something in David's letter.

It was August, and the yellow sun cut like an axe through the tense air of the green valley, but David was not conscious of the heat— only of the sharp pounding of his heart.

He passed the two stores, the four weather blackened houses, then crossed the log bridge to the Baptist Church where he sank panting on a rough pine step. He waited, letting his unseeing eyes follow a white butterfly dipping lazily among the green weeds. Very carefully, he tore open the envelope. From the sheet before him, the words shouted:

"Your examination was excellent. You are given the Rybon School for the next two terms." With a woop, David sprang to his feet and darted through the bushes. The village of scattered pig pens and corn patches had ended with the church.

Now David turned his steps sharply to the right and followed the gullied path leading to his father's cabin. His pale face shone and his undernourished body, in baggy trousers and a child's coat, seemed to be pulled forward by the happiness of his blue eyes. Usually he stopped at the upper bend of the trail and leaned for a few minutes against a gigantic hickory. There was always a pain in his chest when the breath came fast.

But today he plunged eagerly up the steep grade, unconscious even of his feet slopping clumsily upon the sharp igneous stones.

"Ma, Ma," he called.

From behind the house - crude and barred by the mountaineers artistry of its natural protection of trees - came a slim woman of thirty-five, her smooth hair caught tightly back from her low forehead and timid eyes.

"Ma," he gulped again, "I got it - the teachin'.They've given me the job at Rybon."

"Lor, Son, I'm that proud." She put her hands on his shoulders. "Yer pa'll be proud too. Now he won't expect so much plowin' and hoein' an all that. My how you've hated it Son." She laughed, but stopped suddenly as though ashamed.

"Just think, Ma" he babbled on, "ther'll be thirty scholars an' nobody to pester me about what to teach 'm. Just wait. Soon I'll be hanging pictures of Washington and Jefferson on the wall. Soon those young rascals will be getting it into their heads that they want to be President."

They both laughed at this. Here was a real joke - the first they had shared in many days.

Finally the opening morning of the summer school term had arrived. Alone, David had spent the previous day cleaning the school house. The desks had been left in disorder, full of papers and apple cores, last winter's mud tracked the floor and the blackboards shone with the deviltry of cartoons. In spite of his weariness, David had enjoyed the work. This was the real beginning of his life and he felt himself baptized with his own yearning. As he polished the grimy panes of glass, he liked to think that he was shining the windows of his soul. The agony he had suffered in his father's corn field was over; before him was the world of thought and mental advancement.

David's pupils arrived on time. On the long rough benches challenged the freshly washed faces of his pupils, ranging in age from six to fifteen. The younger children sat toward the front. At the back of the room lounged the older boys. There was a snicker from the group at the rear and a book fell heavily to the floor.

"I'll have to arrange you better," said David, his voice steady with authority. "You big boys, come sit over here to the left of the little fellows." For a moment there look was insolence. The 'little fellows' nudged each other and looked furtively behind. Suddenly Roth Hummock laughed coarsely.

"The last teacher we'un had," he blurted, looking around to see that his companions were backing him, "we chased off with knives. I guess we ain't aimin' to mind nobody."

For a moment David stood speechless, a slow nausea creeping through his veins. From the back row, the stubborn sun-browned faces and young sinewy arms dared him with the superiority of physical health. His sensitive flesh shrank as from a blow.

His confused gaze now fell upon the cheap print of Washington hanging upon the opposite wall. He noticed that the picture was crooked and remembered how tired his fingers had been when he had driven the nail in place. But the sight of his hero's face, once again the ideal of his school swept over him. And with it came courage, a courage that needs neither whip nor fists.

"Boys," he said, speaking as though he had heard

something quite pleasant, "do you know that we are goin' to need those knives? First inside for sharpenin' pencils, but mostly outside. Suppose everybody come out on the school grounds, I've got some plans you'll be likin'. He pulled his coat importantly about him and walked out.

The younger children followed eagerly, as something of importance was to be uncovered before their eyes. Roth Hummock tried to laugh, but no one noticed him. So grudgingly, then curiously, he slouched out with the others into the yard.

"You see, boys and girls," David pointed to a bare space on the ground, "Every now and then we are going to have a good time here. We are going to have a barbecue."

"A what?" the question came in one gulp from the children.

"Why a barbecue. We'll dig a hole, and get a pig, and roast him right here. And you bet, we'll need plenty 'uv knives to cut him up with, and knives to slice the pickles and onions, and" - David's voice grew very confidential - "I have known boys to take a knife and cut off a pigs tail and roast it special. Let me see your knife, Ted."

"Here's mine."

"And mine."

"And mine." A row of shining blades confronted him.

"That's fine. Now keep up the good work boys. We'll be needin' them soon - after good work, remember; — A barbecue is a kinder prize."

David was, of course, Kate Fort, as she began teaching in the fall of 1903. It was a triumph when she thought of the bar-b-que and asked the boys to bury their knives. She was mightily relieved when they complied. This incident demonstrated one of Kate Fort's great skills; to take an uncomfortable situation or even a misfortune and turn it into something better, even useful.

Arthur Henry Codington
Amtrak 1979
New Jersey

We emerge from the long tunnel under the Hudson River into the bright light of the New Jersey afternoon. This is a state that divides itself between suburban sprawl and the urban centers of New York and Philadelphia, between Jets, Giants and Eagles fans, and between farmlands, marshlands and industrial spaces. The northeast portion of New Jersey is in the opinion of many, a suburb for the metropolis of New York City which looms for miles over the Hudson River from the train window. But farther south, along the coast, are miles of beautiful marshes, and I know that beyond the reach of my window are farmland, mountains and forests. Soon, my view is of wetlands that fit neatly between highways and housing developments. Our first stops are in Newark and Elizabeth, towns formed by my Codington ancestors. Their influence is now found only in occasional town and street names, an old preserved graveyard or a historical society.

I'm including a short biography of Arthur Codington whose northern roots date to the founding of Boston in 1630 and of New Jersey not many years after, since Kate and Arthur were married nearly sixty years. They celebrated their fiftieth anniversary in September of 1958. (I am the only grandchild who was present, but not at the party or in the family photographs. I was napping, comfortably asleep upstairs.) The Codingtons had six children and fourteen grandchildren. Of the fourteen girls he had produced in just two generations Arthur quipped, "Well it's a woman's world, and I've done my best to make it one."

The Codingtons, originally Coddington, and the branches that married into them, arrived in America with the first Puritans in the Great Migration that began in 1630. By 1670 all their direct ancestors had left Boston and New Haven to create a 'Godly society in the wilderness of New Jersey.' They named it Elizabethtown.

Jumping forward just over one hundred year to the time of the American Revolution - these families, Coddingtons, Bonnells, Peirsons, Coons, Mills and Prudens - had prospered on farms and in various professions. Their's are the farms of New Jersey, that supplied the food for Washington's army at Morristown for two winters. These farmers were known for supplying food, but also young men, as nearly every family sent at least one or two to fight with the Continental forces. The women, wives, daughters and young children, stayed on the farms not only to supply the army at Morristown, but to protect their land during the forage wars. The name given to the American skirmishes against the Hessian and English armies for supplies and animal forage.

Another century forward and census records show that Augustus Codington, (the D was dropped from their name in the mid nineteenth century), was a farmer and a carpenter. The same census lists his brother as being in the "lumber business." Just after this, Augustus and his wife, Mary Elizabeth (Bonnell) Codington, left Liberty Township, New Jersey and moved with their young son, Eugene, to Towns, Telfair County, Georgia. Augustus, took good advantage of the abundant yellow pines and with his background in carpentry, he opened a sawmill and lumber company.

The lumber company prospered, and soon Augustus and Mary were able to buy property on Vineville Avenue in Macon. Their two other sons were born there, Arthur in 1883, and Herbert soon afterward.

Arthur was quick with puns and quick to judge, but to those he loved, he was irresistible and fun. A product of the deep south, where he was born and educated, his parents' deep New England roots gave him a work ethic and a rigid morality. It could also be said that it gave him a unique knowledge of the opposite, as he wrote poems with naughty double entendres that often embarrassed his children.

My grandfather Arthur, whom we called Poppy, was a precocious young man. He graduated from Mercer College at seventeen, Mercer Law at nineteen, and then went on to receive a second law degree from George Washington University Law School. He was admitted to the Georgia bar at nineteen in 1902. He was rarely satisfied with a job or a task for long, becoming bored and easily, and disgusted when things were not going well. This dissatisfaction led to the family moving, to Atlanta, Florida and then back to Atlanta, as Arthur sought professional satisfaction.

One summer Arthur took some time away from his law office in Macon to accompany his parents and stay a few days at their summer cottage in Mt. Airy. The Codington Cottage was just down the hill from Mountain Hall, and it was inevitable that shy, gracious and secretly bold Kate would meet the tall, intelligent man with the quick sense of humor. It was not inevitable that they would fall in love, but of course they did.

The first wedding, Arthur Codington and Kate were married September 10, 1908: again one of Mother's parties; Mountain Hall echoing with the sound of wedding bells; young folks all grown up; a White Cake for the first time with a ring and thimble in it. I remember so well the bridal supper, the menu, the decorations.

Susan Fort Redfern in Lulah Ellis Fort, a
memoir of her mother

I do not have a sweet love story for Kate and Arthur as I do for her parents, but there is no doubt that they had a deep love that thrived and grew for nearly sixty years.

They took their wedding trip in the high mountains of Balsam, North Carolina, a walking tour that was to last for a few weeks. On the trip, Kate wrote home to her mother: "Arthur has spent the better part of each day trout fishing." She later said that she almost packed up and went home.

To those who knew him Arthur Codington was a "character." During the first world war, after having been convinced that a father of three ought not join the army, he opened a business college where he taught shorthand and typing. His oldest daughters were among his first students. Catherine, in a conversation, told me that she could still take shorthand, but could read not a word back.

Arthur was never satisfied with monotony, and a law practice that required driving over back roads to see clients was just that, so he spent as much time as he could on the great loves of his life, his hobbies and his poetry. His hobbies included: fish, at times: tropical, and at others: edible; he studied phrenology, the psuedo-science of reading the shape of the head to reveal character; he studied and practised the then - new, science of testing children for various abilities - his own were guinea pigs. Later in life, he took up flower photography. My father, who inherited his father's vast collection of slides, wondered what he was to do with hundreds of photographs of camellias, a particular favorite. The answer was to leave them around to become my brother's problem. He asked the same question, but time and mold have answered it.

Fish

The years the Codingtons lived in Coral Gables,
Florida Arthur bred tropical fish. He had tanks all over
the house and porch, augmented with pools in the
backyard. Once, as I walked in the door after just
arriving home from college at Christmas time, expecting
to be greeted by father with his usual warmth, Poppy
ushered me onto the sunporch, announcing in a stage
whisper, "ssshhh, the fish are breeding."

Catherine Shafer, Personal Correspondence, 1979

The one hobby Arthur maintained throughout his life, was his love of words and although he was never as accomplished as Kate, many of his poems are lovely, and a few were published in

"Georgia Magazine". After he became thoroughly tired of a private legal practice, he became Court Reporter for the Georgia Supreme Court and Court of Appeals. He worked there for many years. On his retirement from his position with the Courts in 1956, the record stated:

COURT OFFICIAL RETIRING —BUT HE WON'T BE IDLE

Arthur H. Codington, recorder for the Supreme Court and Court of Appeals for the past seventeen years, will retire on July 31. Codington, who has been a "watchdog of the King's English" in the court findings, smiled happily when asked about his work over the years. "You can quote me on this," he said. "Now take it down exactly. I don't want to hurt anyone's feelings. "Say, 'although law assistants are perfect, and the judges are super-perfect, (that has a hyphen in it), the typewriters have a way of slipping now and then.'"

"There," he said, "that won't offend anyone."

A sample of Arthur Codington's poetry:

Zests Of Earth

When I who long have loved all radiant flesh,
The press of passion, cling of soft embrace,
Shall find myself released from carnal mesh
And warm lips turn aside from this cold face,
Let no free spirit writhe beneath a lash
For sins that are themselves the penal rue.
But if some lone star's kindly ray or flash

Transmute or astralize the residue,
Or if by mercy cleansed, no virtue crowned,
A soul may rise and breathe pure fragrancies,
To savors faint but lingering ever bound,
Could I forget those mortal vagrancies?

Let being, then, uncleft' from lusty mirth,
Resurge eternally with zests of earth.

Pure Fragrancies and Mortal Vagrancies, 1968

Children

Lollipop

Away with that gun!
Behave yourself!
Who said I had lollipops
High on the shelf?
Oh, maybe just two,
Or only just one.
Why lemon I guess,
Or strawberry red.
Look out, you brute,
Please, please don't shoot!
What's that you said
You'll kill me dead,
You'll sizzle a bullet

Right into my head?
Oh, how could I spank,
Or send you to bed,
But cringe to your rank, You mighty and strong
Old Hop-a-long.
Here, hand me that pistol
And come let's swap
You give me a kiss
For a lollipop.

Unpublished, around, 1923

Children were always enchanted by Kate and sensed in her a kindred spirit. She knew exactly what to say to every child, to receive the maximum cooperation and respect. She treated children, her own, and those of others, as guests and expected them to behave as such. Instead of yelling an order such as, "close the door," she would ask, "Mimi, would you please shut the door?"

Next door neighbor in Atlanta, Emily Hightower, was kind enough to tell me a few stories about living next door to the Codingtons as she grew up.

She understood the quirks of childhood and adolescence. My own adolescence was particularly painful, and the few times those years when she saw me in a bad mood she was understanding, instead of fighting, stood firm and gave me something to push off from. She could bear teenagers because of her inexhaustible energy and her ability to turn everything around. She had the turn of phrase. That could turn everything around. That was the magical thing. She never answered anybody back, she turned the phrase around and made something creative out of it."

I would add that the turn was always kind, never cruel, sarcastic or teasing.

The Moon-Fairy
(a lullaby)

A winsome wee Fairy lives up in the Moon
Hush you, Honey, my Dove
Her laugh is a silvery croon;
Rock - a - bye, Dearie, my Love
She climbs, a ladder
Of cobwebs and pearl,
And presses a kiss on the gold of your curl,
Then upward she flutters with shimmer and
        whirl,
Leaving a token to keep
A smile on the lips of Baby, my Girl,
A sparkle of beauty to twinkle and twirl
In dreams as you nestle asleep.

Macon Daily Telegraph, Dec. 12, 1915.

Nicknames

In gray and chill of twilight time,
Between the dew and frost,
I counted seven silver stars —

Each separate and lost.
I called them Jerry,
Sue, and Mae, Clarisse and Annabelle.
And Polly too and Sailor-boy.
They promised not to tell;
But fluttered down upon the dark,
A dozen, then a score,
And flocked like pigeons flock —
A million round my door.
0 never call them Jupiter,
Or Sirius, or Mars.
Such formal words confuse and pain
And make them frozen stars.
But call them little children's names;
Then watch them laugh and run.
They'll twinkle round your chimney-top
Till rising of the sun.

Shod with Light, 1966

Ballad of The Briar Rose

What matter briars sharp as steel,
Filling the mote, climbing the tower?
For I, a prince of gay romance,
Shall break the magic power.

The brambles part.
I enter, pass
The King, the Queen, the snoring Groom
The Cook who slapped the Stable boy,
The Fool, his legs about the broom.

On, on they asleep, or so pretend.
Who knows? Perhaps they fake a nap -
To seize my gold the royal pair
Have laid a trap!

So what?
I laugh and climb the stairs,
And wander halls and rooms galore,
Till in a turret's dizzy height -
Behold a door.

And here I find you, beauteous one,
In mists of spider-web you lie;
But on your lips and through your curls
A sunbeam sparkles roguishly.
I give my kiss. Nor shall I fear
The startled court, the blasting horn
If in your heart, Oh, Briar Rose, I find no other
   thorn.

Shod With Light, 1966

Kate had a wonderful way of introducing children to nature. A walk with her through the woods was to experience religion in its most profound. God was everywhere, in each tiny flower as well as the beauty of the whole. To children these hidden lovely places were caves where fairies might live; then all rodents of an Atlanta park achieved new significance as knights or messengers going quickly on their way.

After Kate and Arthur moved to Macon, they bought a house

on Vineville Avenue, near the Codington parents, and Arthur drove his old Model T over back roads to visit clients who could not come to town. Kate gave music lessons, wrote, and raised her growing family. The children came in pairs; two girls, two boys and then another set of two girls, usually called "the babies". In 1915 and 1916, Kate wrote a weekly column for women and children in the Macon Daily Telegraph. Her column was called "The Candle Flame" or "Leisure Hour". In it she wrote poems and short essays on issues she felt were important to women and their families. I have interspersed them, by topic, throughout this work.

Miss Chameleon

Miss Chameleon lived in an old log. She was just a little Lizard, and her morning dress was the color of her house. This was a great help, for when she took her naps out in the sun, a big Hawk soaring by would say, "that's just a piece of bark." She never cooked dinner. You see, there were plenty of wood-worms in the log. Whenever a Worm crawled by, out would go Miss Chameleon's tongue, and gone would be the Worm. Oh, no, she. had no teeth. She only ate soft insects.

One day, a swarm of Flying Ants with long, gauzy wings came out of the rotten wood. My our little lizard was happy; how she licked them up!

Miss Chameleon's party dress was bright green. She put this on whenever she played on the grass.Then when an Old Snake would crawl by, he would say, "That's just a leaf." Not far from the log was a beautiful lawn, always cool, and fresh.One day Miss Chameleon invited two of her friends to a picnic on the lawn. "Maybe," she said, "we can catch some gnats." The lizards started out.

As soon as they arrived they put on their pretty green dresses. Do you know how they did this? They simply stood in the grass for a minute, and their little brown suits turned green. Off they scampered in the sunshine. My what fun, and such crowds of gnats.

A big Tom Cat lay watching them from behind a bush. Look! There he sprung high in the air, and, pounce! He caught Miss Chameleon by the tail.

Oh yes, our little lizard's tail grew back. It took a long time, though, and while it was growing she stuck tight to the old log. During the long summer, sometimes she would put on her party dress and frisk about the woods. But she never gave another picnic on the lawn.

Macon Daily Telegraph, Dec. 26, 1915

The Turtle's Riddle

I went to the pond to find what the old turtle would tell me. He was lying on the sand, and when he saw me coming, he drew his head and tail tight up in his shell, till he looked like a speckled drum.

"Now don't be afraid," I said poking him gently with a stick, "I've come to ask you a question."

"Ask away," he said sticking out his neck and squinting at me with his little weepy eyes.

"Well," I replied, "I would like to know which you love best— the land or the water."

He thought a long time, then he shook his big ugly noggin. "It's hard to tell," he said, "you see, when I want to be cool, I swim in the water; and when I want to be hot I sit in the sun. When I want to eat flies, I lie on the sand; and when I want to eat water-bugs I jump in the pond." "One day," he continued dreamily, "there were four of us turtles dozing on a log. Suddenly it began to rain, and quick as a snap, the last one of us slid into the water to keep dry."

"Now," he said, "which do you think that I like best-the Water or the Land?"

I had to give up. Which do you think?

Macon Daily Telegraph, Mar. 26, 1916

The Flight of the Monarch Butterflies

Just a month ago, not far from the Blue Ridge Mountains. I was caught in a swarm of Monarch Butterflies. It was a wonderful afternoon. The sky shone deep and clear, without a breath of breeze to stir the warm freshness of the late September air. I stood on a high hill, and could see for miles and miles over the tree tops to the mountain ridges beyond. The world stretched green beneath, with here and there the flash of a red black-gum tree, or the glittering plumy heads of a field of goldenrod.

Suddenly like a shower of autumn leaves, light as soap bubbles, floating, sailing, drifing about me, came the Butterflies. Thousands upon thousands of them passed, waving their wings in the long shafts of sunlight, silent as the ripples of a river. They did not hurry. They moved onward gently, happily, as though keeping time to wondrous music calling them ever southward to the far away land of flowers.

Where are you going, you lovely creature? I asked of one whose wings nearly brushed my face. She whirled a moment about my head, then lighted upon a twig nearby. So I began to talk, and she seemed to answer me, "Where are you going?" I repeated.

"I am fleeing from the cool days," she said, "so soon to come creeping from the north, and I seek the country where the Milkweed keeps fresh and juicy." "What do you want with Milkweed?" I demanded. "Why you see," and she looked important. "We must lay our eggs on the leaves of Milkweed, for Baby Caterpillars hatched from these eggs are royal children, and they must have the proper food." "Do they know that they are royal?" I replied smiling.

"Oh yes, indeed!" and Madame Butterfly stiffened her feelers.

"When the time comes for each little worm to become a chrysalis," she continued, "he spins about himself a most gorgeous blanket, all pale and green and spangled with gold. Then when his long sleep is over, out he breaks from his jeweled cover, spreading his wings, red-bronze, striped with black velvet, shiny with black polka-dots, and sails away with the wind, a real Monarch. Good-bye."

"Won't you ever come back?" I cried, seeing her glide like a dew-drop from the twig, then flit out into the open twilight. "Oh, yes," she called. "Many of us will return next summer, not in flocks like this, of course, but we will still be looking for Milkweed."

It was growing dark, and the butterflies were still thronging by, but I noticed that they were clustering in the trees, to await, I suppose, the early call of the sun.

Macon Daily Telegraph, Nov. 19, 1916

Motherhood

This essay was written in the 1930s. In it, Kate answered what must have been a common question for a mother with six children.

The Big Family

"How do you do it?" my friend asked me. "How do you keep house, help your children with their studies, give music lessons, sew, belong to clubs, write poetry and play cards with your husband? And besides all this, how do you stimulate so much affection, health and happiness in your home?"

After twenty-five years of experience, I am asking myself these same questions. I am wondering what is that essence of living and thinking which successfully perpetuates the familiar picture of little brothers and sisters, measuring themselves, like stair steps, against the nursery wall.

I acknowledge that among the upper classes, the big family is not only old-fashioned, but almost obsolete; that like most past institutions, it has become interesting rather than necessary. I, therefore, have no desire to reverse the wheel of time and advise young people to undertake the bearing and rearing of many children. But drawing from my own experience, as a member of a large family and as mother of six young people, I would like to show under what conditions, even today, the big family is giving to the world its well rounded and superior type of individual.

Many of us remember when our leading citizens began to relegate child rearing to the poorer classes. Barricading their conscience with platitudes of the economist and the birth control fanatic, they have watched with wry pity and no regret while the social untouchables have made a success of populating the country. If either the very rich or the very thrifty had assumed the responsibility of producing the nation's yearly crop of youngsters, I doubt if the result would have proven more advantageous. The types of mind usually accompanying extreme wealth, extreme frugality and extreme poverty are equally unsuited to the rearing of normal children. The superficial dignity and mental laxity of the brown stone mansion, the material ideal and hidden militarism of the "chase penny" establishment, and the privation and stunted growth of the homes of poverty, each develops its own deformity.

Our present mechanical age contributes little to the inner life of the child. Man was created with joyous rather than useful instincts; and as his number decreases in the modern adult group, he often suffers the loneliness of an alien.

Of course, no one is to blame for this. In planning their families, parents have a right to consult their pocketbooks. So if an only child finds his home life uncongenial, his father and mother artificial, the only available remedy for his condition is our improved school system. Yet there are some parents, even in this age of depression, who are willing to gamble their last penny on this greatest of all adventures - the big family.

This article is written as an effort to explain this type of parent. For it is not the children who should be eliminated, but the parents who should be selected.

I would suggest as necessary traits for the fathers and mothers of big families: enthusiasm, idealism, artistic talent, sense of humor and above all a fair amount of impracticability. By impracticability, I mean the faith to plan results without apparent means for their accomplishment. Persons possessing these qualities are never morbid, so usually have good health and the courage to survive emergencies.

I number among my friends about a dozen such parents. These men and women have a cultural background, high mental ability, a smile of understanding upon their lips, a dream in their eyes, while on their backs shines either a made-over dress, or a coat of several winters.

The mothers are not women of the large, square build. They are small-boned, with the clean cut features of the artist, and possess a stimulating personal attractiveness. Their homes are not patterns of system, but their houses are not disorderly. There is a friendly cooperation between furniture and inmates, an adaptability to change, amazing to the uninitiated guest.

In five minutes, I have seen a living room turn from a study to a vaudeville stage, the piano swing from Moonlight Sonata to Chop Sticks, and the kitchen emerge, from the quiet atmosphere of stewing prunes and steaming rice to a pandemonium of burnt fudge and sticky fingers.

And, if occasionally things are left topsy turvy, and the youngsters bolt for a lark on the beach, these mothers are not ruffled. They probably suggested the escapade themselves. They accept the extra work with a smile, unconsciously proving that it is fret, not work, which destroys mothers as well as other women. The too precise woman tires easily and becomes nervous over unfinished detail. The mothers of whom I write are able to shut the door upon temporary disorder, and walk out in their gardens for rest of mind and body. They know that tomorrow the children will undertake their duties with renewed energy; that nagging blinds cooperation.

These parents transcend life rather than succumb to its difficulties. They see happiness evolving from temporary distress, and find in their own souls the joy necessary for the rearing of a family. Theirs is a perennial youth, adaptable and eager for change. They are willing to don the garb of Pan, and pipe with their children beneath the green branches; are willing to count stars and consider them more valuable than dollars. Not that money is unimportant— a substantial amount must be earned. But the difference between the normal expense of a large and small family is not as staggering as is usually supposed. The cost for individual housing, food and heat are less in the larger group. Clothes are passed down, opportunities are shared, helpful friends are more numerous. The parents of whom I write work hard. And because they are units in the family partnership and are treated as individuals, the children earn when they can without coercion.

It is not the minimizing of money, but the

emphasizing of more permanent values which sustains the morale of a large family in spite of vicissitudes. Of course this emphasis must come first from the parents.They must realize that when beauty, truth and self-respect come soon in the life of a child, love of money can never become an absorbing passion, nor material gain be more than a tool for higher accomplishment. In such a home, motives and tendencies are considered rather than sudden or incidental passion. There is much love, great patience and little punishment. It is in these impractical families, unencumbered by too much materialism, that children best develop a normal sense of responsibility and a sane attitude toward life.

I was brought up in a big family, and I remember that our happiness was as much affected by an honor won at college by a brother or sister as by the success of a peach crop upon which our support more or less depended. But we survived gloriously, even when times were hard, because our parents were of the type which, in those days, could borrow on its own integrity, and because of mental superiority was always able to pay.

We had a friend, an old gentleman, who at eighty-three belonged to a bicycle club. I have never known anyone with such enthusiasm for life nor with such a contagious, happy laugh. Between his glowing adventures, on foot and on his wheels, his joy was to lecture upon the glories of heaven. With his care-free mind, how he managed to bring up, almost single handed his five daughters - intellectual, substantial women - he scarcely knew - moves, experiments, plunges.

Where he failed, the daughters learned to

supplement. Through years, colorful with ups and downs, the girls learned self-reliance, gained social prominence, and with him learned to laugh. Until his death, he walked with the stride of a young man, his happiness defying the ills to which the human race is heir. Trials which would have broken others, he never realized. Because of the combination of his attributes, as a man and as a father, he was a paramount success.

I lived for seven years in a South Florida town. Among the choice citizens were several families, each including six or seven children. In the midst of her household duties, the mother of every group carried on her music or art, and held a responsible position in one or more clubs. These women were not only eager to create through their children, but recognized responsibility to their own talents. They did not fret because occasionally Susie did not practice her violin, or because Jimmy made a C on his report card. But I lived among them long enough to see their Susies and Jimmies become leaders in the musical and intellectual lives of their contemporaries.

These women were able to turn from a long vigil beside a sick child, and with a smile, serve tea to a casual guest or put a few telling strokes on a watercolor. Their spiritual adjustment was like a shining armor against distress, their universal vision and personal dream a victory in defeat.

The principal of an elementary school, attended at the time by three of my children, asked that I give her my method of child training. Her teachers, she said, attributed my children's superiority to better home atmosphere. I told her that I had no method unless it was the ability to see essentials beyond the stumbling blocks.

My husband and I are in our early fifties. Two of our daughters are married. The eldest is an outstanding musician. Having received her first instruction at home, she was able to win a scholarship and study under a famous musician. The second daughter is doing literary work while managing a new home and a new baby. My two boys are both fine athletes and are planning to help themselves through college, one with shorthand, the other with the trumpet.

The little girls twelve and ten, are capable, ambitious children. It is to their work and enthusiasm that the family is indebted for our beautiful garden.

We live in a Southern community where culture and home standards come first. We make no apologies for our shabby car or inexpensive parties. If a friend passes on to us a box of pretty, outgrown garments, we are delighted and feel no inferiority. We know that we can return such kindness in other ways. Life has been, with us, the sharing of material and spiritual blessings. What we receive we use, and hand to the next in line with the regularity of the old fashioned bucket brigade, whether it be a teapot, a table or a pair of sturdy overalls.

Unpublished about 1930-

THE KING OF WORLDLY WISDOM

The King of Worldly Wisdom issued a
    proclamation that at each Stage of Human
    Life he would bestow the gift most desired.

First came the Children: "Give us Growth," they
    asked-

And the King gave them Rules.
With these Rules, the Children became cramped,
    artificial and lost the fresh Spontaneity with
    which they were created.

Second came the Maidens: "Give us Beauty,"
    they asked-
And the King gave them Clothes.
With clothes, the Maidens learned the love of
    finery.
They became vain, envious, worshipers of
    flattery.

Third came the Young Men:
"Give us power," they asked-
And the King gave them Money.
With Money, they began to scheme brother
    against brother, piling up possessions,
    stifling honest competition, selling their
    souls for selfish gain.

Last came the Old People.
"Give us Peace," they asked
And the King took away their Work.
Then the Old People passed their days in aimless
    monotony and neglect, wearying of life that
    lingered with them.

Macon Daily Telegraph, January 32, 1916

It seems hard to remember a time when child labor was the norm, and not all children had the luxury of attending school. In Macon, watching her children play at the park near the college where Arthur was teaching secretarial skills for the War Department, Kate met a fellow mother and poet, Sarah Norcliffe Cleghorn. Cleghorn is known for her poems of protest, most especially on the issue of child labor. Kate, who loved all children and believed each should have a chance to grow to his or her fullest, penned this poem at that time.

CHILDREN'S VOICES
The Cry for Public Education

Oh, the sound of children's voices!
Don't you hear them, calling crying.
From the highland, from the lowland,
From the city and the sea?
They are pleading you to give them
Of the misered truth you're hoarding,
So to save them from the darkness
Of the years that are to be.
Don't you see the little shoulders
Stooped from hoeing in the furrows,
And the pinched and sharpened faces
White from straining in the mill,
While the eager forms implore you
For the manhood that awaits them,
And the baby fingers tear you
In the anguish of their will?
For their feet they would be turning
To the school house, in their yearning,
Which their fathers hewed and founded
With a Nation for a plan;
And they seek but for a corner,

Just to grow beneath the heavens
Straight and strong as God would shape them
Into woman into man.
Don't you hear them, moaning, sobbing,
On the farmland, on the wildland,
For their labor that is squandered
In the days so cramped and poor?
From the race they would be running
Would you bar them ere the starting?
While the forms of stunted children
Block the future at your door.

Macon Daily Telegraph, Jan. 23, 1916

The six children were born within fourteen years of each other, so it would stand to reason that at least one of Kate's stories would be about a birth. The events in this story happened at the birth of her fourth child, Februrary1920. The world-wide influenza pandemic of 1918-1919 had persisted. This was the first of her children born in a hospital, which was true for most mothers using the new maternity wards. This was also true for the nurses working in these new facilities. Birth certificates were also new that year in Bibb County, Georgia.

Abraham, Issac and Jacob

Skillfully, the nurse tucked a blanket about my shivering knees.
"No, no" I gasped, "it's the sheets. They're wet."
"Sure," she flashed on me her velvet-blue eyes, "everybody's got it, the laundry help same as the rest of

us. Hold on a few minutes the sheets will be dry." Her violet blue eyes flashed reproach.

This was soon after World War I, when not only our town, but much of the inhabited globe groaned under a devastating epidemic of influenza. The small crowded hospital where I had come for my confinement was hard hit. Nurses and orderlies grew livid at their posts. And the maternity ward - a new experience for many of us Southern women, accustomed to bearing our babies at home, was far from adequate.

Much of our distress was caused by the newly born.

These tiny creatures, as though sensing the general unhappiness, pervaded the floor with endless protest, resembling the tones of a scratchy fiddle.

"There's one baby that never stops," I complained to Miss Simmons the next time that she came in, bearing the pink wooly blanket containing my, so far, comfortable son.

"His doctor's out of town, and his mother's too ill to nurse him." Mechanically she placed the squirming little bundle beside me, watching with cold eyes as I pulled back my laces and ribbons and made ready for his feast.

"How terrible," I gasped, looking with sudden alarm at my offspring, so greedily beautiful in his prosperity.

"She's a Greek woman, can't speak a word of English. I don't know which scares her most, the thermometer or the kid."

With this remark, Miss Simmons straightened out my bed, rearranged the flowers on the dresser and a bit later bore my sleeping son off to the nursery.

About midnight she reappeared, bringing a glass of chocolate.

"Did you ring?" she asked icily.

"That baby's still crying," I moaned. "Can't somebody do something, fix a formula or..."

"I told you that baby's doctor's out of town. None of us nurses can take the responsibility."

"Lord, have mercy," I groaned. And because there was nothing I seemed able to do, I let a big tear roll down my cheek.

It was a long time before I really slept. My head ached, and the crying of the hungry infant tore at my nerves as well as my heart-strings. When I opened my eyes, the room was bright with sunshine, and Miss Simmons, in immaculate, white was standing beside the window, my red carnations glittering like tiny frames beside her. For a few moments, I lay in a happy doze wondering vaguely how a trained nurse could be either so beautiful or so cold.

Then I remembered ."Oh, that baby, he's stopped crying! What's happened?" "The baby's dead." "Dead, no, no!" "Yes, dead." Suddenly the world went black before me. Here we were, mothers, nurses, all listening, and yet we had done nothing.

"Miss Simmons that baby didn't have to die, and you know it." With that I really began to weep.

Sternly Miss Simmons approached me with her ever present thermometer.

"Some babies live and some babies die," she said, "That's all there is to it."

"You brute," I shrieked inwardly, "And you don't even care."

And now another baby tuned up - his voice frantic, desperate like that of his predecessor.

"Miss Simmons," I pleaded, as night returned, "don't let that baby die too. Is it his mother?"

She nodded, "Her nipples are cracked and swollen.

The baby can't nurse."

"And the baby's doctor?"

"He says it's better to wait a day or so till the mother's better. He believes in breast-milk for infants."

"But suppose he won't be here – suppose he has flu. Have you thought of that? Then you'll be throwing that child out with all the other withered flowers."

"Miss Simmons, bring me that baby. You know that I've got plenty of milk."

"Against orders," she snapped, and started for the door. "Don't go you've got to listen." I caught her apron. "This crime will be on both of us, on you and on me."

"Remember what Christ said about his little ones. And remember about that mill stone that's going to be hung about your neck!"

I shall never forget the tiny skeleton, which a few minutes later Miss Simmons uncovered beside my pillow - the legs scarcely bigger than my finger, the claw-like hands, the tight yellow skin, the bald head with its pathetic fringe of hair. But the jaws! How they grabbed me, and held me, and oh, how they nursed!

On and on they worked, until the stomach, barely hidden by the cheap hospital garment, swelled up like a toy balloon.

On and on until peace enveloped us and the little one slept on my arm.

Miss Simmons entered softly. And when she lifted up the baby, to my amazement I saw tears streaming from her violet-blue eyes.

"Abraham, Isaac and Jacob," she murmured, trying to smile. "Oh, yes," I laughed, glad to turn my emotions into history. "Thank you Miss Simmons, you're right - Abraham, Isaac and Jacob."

"The hospital shall never know," I said a few minutes later, for she lingered in that speechless tenderness, inspired only by the need of a little child.

"I'm not afraid," she said, and flashed that look of joyful conspiracy we all love. And again I thought her beautiful.

Unpublished 1930-

It was baby John who was born in 1920, in the middle of that epidemic. He was the fourth, child following Tallulah, Catherine, and Arthur, (Artie) and the last to be born in Macon. In 1921, Arthur was offered a position as a law clerk in Atlanta, and the family moved to the capital. Mary and Emily were born there in 1923 and 1925.

Busy with six children, Kate did not have time for writing or music, but determined to find a way, she rose each morning at five in order to have a few hours for herself.

Mother's secret to ready energy was the ten minute nap. After lunch, or if a child were sick, as soon as he rested, she would lie down. Like the eastern masters she was able to relax completely, in an easy doze for a few minutes and awake totally refreshed. In this way she could go on for as long as an illness lasted, napping whenever she had the chance.

Catherine Shafer, Person Correspondence, 1979

Miami Daily News, Sunday, November 13, 1932
Miami Muse - A weekly column devoted to South
Florida's Poets Conducted by Vivian Yeiser Laramore
(Poet Laureate of Florida)

...Mrs. Codington is an active member of the local branch
of the American League of Penwomen, and received
their sonnet prize given in celebration of National Poetry
Week of this year. She should forever silence those who
have a habit of saying that a woman must choose
between a career and a family. Certainly Kate Fort
Codington had been successful in fostering both.

But even a woman with such energy, needed to admit to her
limitations. She wrote about the conflict between civic
engagement and mothering.

The Frog Pond

Norma Trench turned over on her pillow. Her eyes
were closed but her nerves were acutely awake. She
was listening to year old Binny stumbling among his
playthings. Why should a baby wake so early, after
hours of croupiness which had broken pitifully into the
rest of a hot night?

On the sleeping porch, the four older children slept

noiselessly in the double beds. The two girls had been to a party the evening before. It would be a shame to disturb them, but she must have help. Norma's eyes sought the clock only fifteen minutes before time to put on the cereal. Lord, could anyone but a mother yearn so for the rest of fifteen minutes, or in fifteen minutes be able to regain so much strength?

It was to Jim, the ten year old boy to whom Norma finally appealed. "Jim, darling, keep Binny a little while, Mother must sleep - just a little while darling." She felt like a criminal when the touseled head of Jim appeared at the door - but oh the relief.

That afternoon Norma was to make an address in the Chapter House before the Society of National History. The orator from Vermont had disappointed the committee, so Norma had been asked. The town had not quite forgotten that Norma also was distinguished; only a few years before, she had written and produced an historical pageant.

"Perhaps," Norma would sometimes think, "if there were not so many children and the thousand and one distractions of home life, I might have gone on, might have written something worthwhile." She would look at her family and murmur, "When they are grown I shall have time - even when they all go to school." But just then, and always when this restless mood attacked her, Binny would conquer. He would come toward her, crawling in his one-sided fashion, his dimples shining, and spouting out his chuckling laugh. "Bless your heart. Baby Binny," and she would hoist him to her shoulder. "Why should you ever grow up, or you or you?" as the brown and gray eyes of the other children would meet hers.

But today she was an automation so far as the

family was concerned. Every hour she would slip upstairs to practice her speech. She was not to read it. This was to be her opportunity to regain her prestige in the community.

The theme of her talk was not new but it was her own. Patriotism does not consist in one hundred percent Americanism. Was it not the duty of The Society of National History to preserve the vision of Washington, and avoid both foreign entanglements and national conceit?

At noon Baby Binny developed a temperature. "Children, what shall I do, how can I leave him?" The half-day maid was sullen when asked to nurse and complained of dinner.

"But Mother," interposed Jane's confident little voice, "Lou and I are here. We won't go to the picture show, and Jim can help. Please don't worry, Mother."

Both of the younger children were crying while Norma dressed. Little John had burnt his finger and Baby Binny refused to stay in bed.

"Don't worry, Mother," again Jane's voice trailed above the hubbub; "they'll be good as soon as you go."

It was two thirty when Norma stepped out on the sidewalk. She had taken Binny's temperature - one hundred and two. "The castor oil will fix him." She tried to reassure herself but the tragedy of it lingered. She condemned herself as frivolous, treacherous.

The sun flared as a surprise in her face. How green the trees for August! Submerged in her speech and in the children, for days she had scarcely been conscious of the outside world. As she turned the corner her mind grew acutely clear. She saw herself as two women, one domestic, disheveled with a crying baby in her arms; the other as artist, surrounded by the flowers of the Chapter House. But thoughts of Binny prevailed. Why should she leave her sick child? What did self-satisfied women need with a message? They should be at home cooking their dinners.

The Chapter House was in reality an old Colonial Home, too large for its neighborhood of cheap bungalows, so bought for a fraction of its value. The downstairs partitions had been torn down, making a fair sized auditorium. Today a large flag draped the door.

Only a few of the members had arrived. Miss Olsmith gushed from the door and clutched Norma with her bony fingers "Our distinguished speaker, proud of you." There was a jealous gleam in her narrow, black eyes. She always wore plumes on her overlarge hats and lace that had been her grandmother's. How could families peter out into such specimens as Miss Olsmith?

The officers loomed about, their dresses mauve, and lavender. How suave these women, how patronizing. Suddenly Norma felt foolishly young and inexperienced. "It is because of their tongues," she raged inwardly, "Mine's not oiled to give flattery."

Beside the row of officers, Norma seated herself upon the platform, and watched the women come in. She knew most of them, of course. Why did they come? Few of them were literary or interested in national problems. There was Mrs. McVail - she scarcely knew the difference between the Middle and Western States. Was a little social prestige worth all this sacrifice of time and money? Now the women were making advances toward each other with their shy diplomacies. Woman's conquest of woman. Here was the secret of the modern club. The old civilization of women's charm centered about a man, where was that?

In walked Lucy Gilbert. Lucy really possessed brains and enthusiasm, and, thought Norma, she's lovely under her picture hat. The atmosphere seemed clear. Norma leaned back in her chair and smiled. The meeting opened: national hymn, prayer, secretary's report, report of the committees, business. There was much to discuss, primarily whether or not the plumbing in the building should be remodeled, and the ugly exposed pipes and roachy corner-lavatories made to give way to modern, sanitary fixtures. This was Miss Olsmith's opportunity. In her mincing voice she talked and talked, her black eyes shooting tiny vindictive flames about the hall. Norma thought of a terrier with a bone. My, would she never turn it loose? Mrs. Ainsworth of the other side of the hall would not be outdone. "Madam President," and she would spring up, "economy is modern and practical."

"But Madam President," Miss Olsmith's voice was shrill, "the glory and standard of the Society must not be tarnished by a sloppy kitchen floor. Think of the first cold snap!" What were they saying? Norma's head whirled. Sudden visions of Binny flooded her. She saw him crawling to the sidewalk, his cheeks flushed, his nose running. Would they come to her speech? Would they never let her go? Lord, if she had only known how cruel woman could be, not cruel, perhaps, but stupid. There was Mrs. Ainsworth again. Norma gripped the sides of her chair.

It was getting late. Shadows fell blue across the vases of tall flowers. Yes, and the light over the auditorium was green, green through the oak leaves of the trees against the windows, green like the peel near Druken where Norma was born - Druken - tiny lakes of lily pads. Her speech? No, she must keep her mind from that, she must not grow nervous. Besides there was to be music first - some more patriotic songs and a piano solo. But after all, what was the use of all this? Cheap emotionalism, that was what these women asked - frogs in a pool, looking with adoration at the stork who would devour them. Green lights through the auditorium and women's eyes blankly shining toward the platform. Yes, the auditorium was the pool and the women the frogs. Greed and Nationalism was the stork, hid in the feathers of a beautiful flag.

The President was talking. What, what was she saying? Norma's mind gasped back to reality. "On account of the lateness of the hour, the music will be the last part of the agenda so that after the talk, given to us by our dear friend, anyone who finds it necessary to do so may leave. And now I will introduce to you one whom you already know, one whose talents have shown forth as a torch before us and whose love for her country is beyond question. Officers, ladies of the National Society, let me introduce to you Norma Elizabeth Trench." There was a flutter of applause.

Norma rose. A cool wind seemed to greet her as she took a few steps toward the front of the platform. Her nervousness was gone. Nothing mattered now. It would all soon be over and she would be at home. Already her speech seemed a thing of yesterday. With perfect composure yet at random she began to talk.

"Madam President, Officers, guests and ladies of the Historical Society, I appreciate my introduction. Not that I am a shining light as our President so graciously suggests, but because this meeting had struck a match to the otherwise dull candlestick of my mind."

"My subject is Americanism. And it is Americanism indeed that our Fathers once hoped to achieve; Americanism, the ideal of Washington. But what type of Americanism have we today? The exalted Americanism of which we boast, or Americanism debased by the poverties of its masses? Are we not blinded to facts by our vanities? Is not the Society of National History but a unit in a delusion? Is not the opening of the Club House a matter of personal aggrandizement? Why are we sacrificing our time, our money? What is the significance of this afternoon?"

Norma stopped. The eyes of the women were fixed unbatting upon her face. There they were - the frogs. She saw Miss Olsmith lick her lips.

"Yes that's it," her voice sang defiantly, "We are frogs, frogs in a pool. Here we are feeding ourselves, fattening, never dreaming that the stork of our own civilization will consume us for its food. Washington and Jefferson," she plunged on recklessly. —

But something had happened - a stone had been thrown into the frog pond. The expression of the eyes was changing, amazement, fury.

Miss Olsmith flung herself to her feet. "Madam President, I protest that such a name as frogs be hurled on the faces of the ladies of the Historical Society." Half a dozen other women were on their feet. There was chaos. The President pounded for order. Norma heard her own voice, harsh, battling against this crowd of women, turned so suddenly hostile. "Silence, Silence." There was no silence.

"Miss Smith," the words of the President rasped above the heads of the crowd, "will you please play 'America'. Let everybody sing!"

Florence, the plump, half-witted daughter of old

Colonel Bell, swayed in the aisle, "Madam President," she shrieked between great gulps of merriment, "don't you mean let the frogs croak!"

Then it was that the tension burst and the hall rocked with laughter - laughter uncontrolled, hysterical - the pent emotion of three hours of unnatural restraint loosed in a deluge. Norma's cheeks flamed. She must apologize. She must tell them that she did not mean this Club more than all clubs. Tell them that Baby Binny was sick and she over wrought. Tell them that frogs, that terrible word, had just slipped from her tongue, because her eyes were so still, so fixed, and the leaves so green against the windows.

She turned to the President, to the Secretary, to the Treasurer. Somebody must be made to understand. As one they turned their backs and sang 'America', desperately, discordantly, as though to save the world from sin.

So that was it, she was beneath their notice. Norma slipped out. Her head was up, but a finger was tremblingly pressed against her lips. She did not see Lucy Gilbert's serious face seeking her among the crowd.

"How is Binny?" she sobbed, as Jane opened the door. "All right, Mother, he's asleep." There he lay, pink and at peace in his little white bed, his breath coming easily between half open lips. The other children stood about, their faces soft with sympathy and admiration.

"How was your speech, Mother?" Their arms stole about her. Then suddenly Norma laughed, laughed till the tears rolled down her cheeks, laughed till little Jane's face twitched and she ran to bring a glass of water.

"Thank you, thank you, dear. Somehow Mother is so very glad to be at home."

When the doorbell rang, the children were already in bed. As though in a dream, Norma ushered into her rather frayed living room, the officers of the Society of National History. There they were, the President, the Treasurer, the Secretary and Lucy Gilbert - Lucy began smiling under her picture hat.

They've come, thought Norma, to pronounce my doom, why bother? It was pronounced this afternoon.

When they were all seated it was Lucy who spoke.

"If I remember rightly," she said, "Aesop's fable did not end with the stork. A few frogs escaped and learned wisdom. We represent those few. Will you be our king and save us from the idiocy of our own bog? In other words, the Society of National History needs new officers. Next month when we present our slate, may your name head the list?"

As the pause was long, Lucy leaned over and patted Norma's hand coaxingly, "Maybe," she said, "the final king of the frog pond was a mother."

"No, no," Norma was laughing as she shook her head."No, no, but thank you. You've helped me tremendously - you'll never know. But I'm no king, just one of the frogs that escaped. A mother frog, yes, and right now I'm busy enough just raising tadpoles."

Unpublished, about 1925

Mountain Mother

She lay quite starved from giving, ever giving
To those maternity had made her care -
But still defying want, she locked her closet
That none might see the larder, stripped and bare.
So proud and so magnanimous her spirt,
She faced her neighbor with merry mood:
And when at last he brought a loaf of barley,
To hide her shame she gave the robins food.

Shod With Light, 1966

Winter Reunion

When children with their children had departed,
And heavy doors had closed upon the flying
Laughter, they the parents, proud, defying
Community among the lonely hearted,
Entered again the room. And though they darted
A glance from toy to book, to cushion lying
About the floor, they made no cry. But vying

As each with each in casualness, slow started
To mount the stairs. And there beside a bed,
That lifted armlike posts against the moon,
They pause, remembering young passion, lost
Buried beneath the winter. Then she said
        Something of tulips.

He more opportune
Sputtered a malediction on the frost.

April Thoughts, 1966

Kate at her graduation from Lucy Cobb Institute, 1903

Lucy Cobb Institute,	Program Notes
Athens, Ga.	
April 7, 1903	1. Two Pianos.
	Andante and Rondo..........................Reinecke
Eight P.M.	Miss Rutherford, Miss Keipp.
	2. Rondo. Op. 51..............................Beethoven
	Miss Rutherford.
	3. Berceuse. ....Chopin
	Miss Fort.
✧	4. Piano Trio.
	Polonaise Brillante...........................Dietrich
	Miss Rutherford, Miss Fort, Miss Keipp.
	5. a. Serenade. ....Strelezski
	b. Lovely May.............................Schumann
Piano Recital	c. Ricordati.................................Gottschalk
	Miss Rutherford.
Given by	6. In the Tavern.......................................Jensen
	Miss Fort.
Miss Katherine Fort	7. Piano Duett.
	Sakontala...Bendel
and	Miss Fort, Miss Rutherford.
	8. Cradle Song...........Jensen
Miss Fannie Rutherford.	Miss Rutherford.
	9. Polonaise. Op 26 No. 1.......................Chopin
	Miss Fort.
	10. Two Pianos.
	Bolero..Reinecke
Facsimile of program	Miss Fort, Miss Rutherford.

Program from Kate's Recital, 1903

Fort children, Will, Kate, Tom, Martha, John is sitting

Lulah Fort's Flower Garden at Mountain Hall, Mt. Airy, Georgia, 1905

The Codington Family, around 1910. Eugene, Arthur, Herbert
Mary Bonnell, and Augustus

Front Parlor of Mountain Hall, Sept 1908

Arthur Codington,1908

Kate and Arthur's Wedding. September 19, 1908 at
Mountain Hall

50th Wedding
Anniversary,
September 1958,
Atlanta, Georgia

The first daughters, Tallulah and Catherine

Kat e around 1918

Kate in Macon with baby Arthur, Catherine, & Tallulah, 1918

Emily, Mary, John and Artie, in Coral Gables, Florida, around 1930.

Kate with 3 daughters and 4 granddaughters, 1950s.

Around 1930
Atlanta, Georgia

Codington Family and Luther Shafer, Catherine's
Wedding, 1933

The author with her family, on the porch at Mt.
Hall, on a very hot July day, 1970.
From left; Kate, Ceil, Dory, Bill and Idy Codington,
Martha Fort Anderson, (Aunt Mar).

Florida: 1926 - 1933

Always anxious to try something different, Arthur Codington decided to move his law practice to the booming state of Florida. He drove down at the beginning of September 1926 to rent a furnished house and move into his office. The family came down by train a few weeks later.

The night they arrived in Miami, on September 18, 1926, also came what is still considered the worst storm of the twentieth century into the Miami area. Now known as the 1926 Miami Hurricane, the recorded winds hovered around 145 mph, at ground level, and the barometer dropped to 930 mbar. These historical measurements may be suspect, but to the Codingtons, this storm on their first night and day in Miami left a lasting memory. Historically, the hurricane and the devastation it brought, broke the Florida land-boom, and led the way to an economic downturn in Florida, years before the rest of the country experienced the Depression.

The Codingtons stayed in Florida for seven years. After living in Miami, they moved to Coral Gables, near the new University of Miami. The famous hurricane also shaped the new school, coming as it did just as the university was scheduled to open. UM teams are called the Hurricanes, named after the storm that Christened the opening.

Ark Of The Everglades

Sweep of the Everglades changeless but moving,
As moves a slow thunder on tepid horizon –
White flame of an egret,

Blue flame of a heron,
And wings of an ibis, whirled up from the
 mangroves!

Thus years are repeated in monotone saw-grass.
With feather on feather,
With evening and morning
As centuries follow the steps of the Father.

Storm broke, and the wind
Became rain, the sky ocean, and then –
Breaker on breaker –
Lashed by the hurricane,
Dashing the bird-bodies
Into the night –
Tattered as rose of the sunrise was tattered.
Over the stillness an ibis is flying –
The ark of some Noah, within her she carries
Eggs of redemption;
New life and new bird-calls
New hope to discover
The gloam of the Everglades,
The umber and umber of shadowless saw-grass
Spoonbill and sandpiper, Pelican skimmer,
Red feather, white feather,
Beryl and silver
Wings to discover
Fresh on the marshland, bright on the water
And deep in the mangroves
Steps of the Father.

Arc of the Everglades, 1975

Kate described that day in these short stories. The first is a memoir, and the second is a fictional work.

Before the Hurricane, the people of Miami hadn't much in common. Most of them had come to South Florida seeking health or fortune, sucked in by the boom or by dreams of prosperity, which lingered long after the hectic bubble had burst.

After the Hurricane, there was but one people, with one bewilderment, one poverty, one hope.

Above the Storm

On Friday, September the 18th, I arrived in Miami with my family. Arthur had rented a charming house in Shenandoah, a residential section of red hibiscus, purple bougainvillea, and orange begonia blossoms. Grapefruit trees grew about the house and filled the vacant lot across the street. The fruit was nearly ripe and clustered in giant pendants, yellow-green, among settings of jade leaves. White curtains blew a greeting at the living room windows, a white apron enveloped the new maid, white clouds piled the rim of the horizon, and white sunlight flooded everything.

Life will be simpler here – thought I. I sat in the loggia listening to the wind through the coconut palm, like the clapping of little hands. I looked ahead into the years; I saw the children stretching up, brown and strong, their backs glistening from the bouyant water - always out with the wind and sky.

"Come,"Arthur interrupted my daydream, "don't

nap, let's take a ride, plenty of time to unpack tomorrow. The maid understands the electric stove and will have dinner ready."

We drove everywhere in the balmy brightness - to the indigo ocean which lay with the white foam of his long locks rippling across the sand. We watched the waves, coy in their entrancing loveliness, never whispering that the hour of their enchantment approached, and that soon they must rise as leviathans and dig themselves caverns in the beach. Little John took a stick... "I will spank Mr. Ocean," he giggled, "He must learn to mind."

We drove home at sundown. Clouds scudded the sky, the wind grew steady. "Do you know," Arthur spoke casually, "a big storm is predicted tonight, a hurricane." "Not really?" I questioned, "perhaps down here all winds are called hurricanes, it looks like rain to me."

After the long first day we went to bed early. A window in our room refused to shut. Oh well, a new house, we would fix it tomorrow. The night deepened. The rain began. The wind became stern, sterner. "Arthur, get a hammer, the rain is drenching the bed." There was no hammer. We strained at the sash as water flooded the room. Then the lights went off. "We'd better go downstairs," grimaced Arthur as he struggled at the window, "I'll lock the door, maybe it will keep the water from running down the steps."

We met the children in the hall, all but baby Emily who slept in my arms. Their eyes were wide and frightened. "Mother, the house shakes, is it an earthquake?" We descended to the living room and lighted a candle. Outside - fury, wind, rain lashing the darkness. Water seeped in around the windows dripping from my room upstairs. "Oh, the poor landlord," moaned the children, "his pretty tables and chairs, Mother, you don't mind if we keep them mopped."After a while the eyes of the workers grew heavy and I piled pillows on the floor. The walls trembled about us. The locked door upstairs rattled like a machine gun, and yet the family slept.

"Mother," my two boys stood above me, "there's a man out there. He's been knocking a long time." I rose wearily. Such stillness, such heaviness, perspiration stood on the faces of the children, still asleep. A tall spare man stood at the door. "Lady, I'm Joe Ludlam your neighbor. The electric wires are down, the wife and I have an oil stove— thought maybe you'd like to come to our place and cook your breakfast."

"Such a storm," I gasped, "Are you a stranger too?"

"...born here." He stretched out his long mahogany arms. "Come on over when you get ready." "I'll take you in the car." Arthur was suddenly beside me. "Then I'll drive around and see the damage."

The car, faced south in the porte cochere. I climbed to the back seat with a coffee percolator and a box of oatmeal. Arthur took the wheel. Then it happened – we had thought the storm was over -- when with a hiss it was back upon us.

There were cries from the house as the hurricane unfurled from its treacherous lull and struck us with its fangs. THE CHILDREN! "Stick by the car, I must go in,"Arthur's words sped by me. The wind threw him to the ground, then tore the screen door from his hands as he managed to scramble to the house. "Thank goodness," I sighed to myself, he's all right, the flashlight signaled that all was well.

There I sat. Shut tight in my ark of safety with the

hurricane swirling around me. Its sound, a long shriek as of escaping steam, no gusts, no diminuendos – just that harsh, high, indomitable note – the mad unison of wind and rain. Later I tasted the rain, it was salty, a mixture of ocean and rainwater, blown three miles inland. The grapefruit, which had survived the night, avalanched about me. Trees blew over, every leaf from every twig shot by like a bullet, or hit the windshield with the sound of metal. I began to move. The car was backing from the porte cochere; instantly I was on my feet – my ark of safety – how did Noah's wife feel when she was left alone to steer?

Inside Arthur was saying, "Mother's all right, she's leaning over, I guess she's saying her prayers." But I was not saying my prayers. I had felt full, physically depressed. But sudden terror cleared my mind and I realized that IF I let go of the brake, I would be killed. Thoughts of the family tore at my heart. As I looked behind me pieces of roof went whirring by, losing themselves in the semi-darkness, beating as blind birds against the iron lamp post. A large blue car, from next door, shot straight as an arrow across the street, crashing into the grapefruit trees. Again my car began to move chattering with its brakes like an old woman."0 God, o God." Yes, Mother was praying.

My help came from the fact that the wheels were turned and as the wind pushed it, the car backed in front of the house, cutting off the force of the wind. I opened and slammed the door and crawled to the porch. "Stick by the car." I had stuck long enough.

A whoop of delight greeted me as I entered the living room – but such a room! Rain swept in furiously, and the house rocked like a three-legged stool. A high stone coping had protected the roof, but under the loosened bars of the steel awning-frames, all the east and south facing windows had caved in. The rest were broken by Arthur with his baseball bat, so that flying glass would not hit the children. The two davenports were pushed against the flapping southern door, and manned by Arthur, the two boys and little Mary, her blond hair messy with rain and worry. The faces of these volunteers were pale, but their eyes triumphant. In a corner crouched my two high school girls, Tallulah and Catherine, holding Baby Emily who kicked and tore at her dress. Her staccato screams could be heard above the storm. "If the house begins to go, Arthur," my voice sounded far away. "Let us run to the grapefruit trees. We can hold on to the roots. The wind's less dangerous than concrete blocks." But the house did not go, and the storm grew no worse. I took off Emily's dress, her nerves relaxed and she slept.

"Poor Mr. Hilburn, see how we've ruined his house, I mopped till the door busted in," ten year old Artie grinned self-consciously. Little John mopped his face. "This old Hurricane's a whopper, but he ain't a-going to knock us down. Look at me hold this sofa." Then I smiled. We all smiled. Soon we were shouting jokes at each other across the din.

We were experiencing the exhilaration of great danger. Little Emily had shed the only tears.

It was two o'clock in the afternoon before it was all over. Suddenly the quaking, rattling, roaring ceased. Light streamed palely over the sea of the living room, where overstuffed chairs huddled like stranded whales in sodden misery. Baby Emily lay curled in the one dry spot, just at the turn of the staircase. For a while we collapsed about her. It had been a bit hard – all in forty-eight hours – to travel a thousand miles, descend two thousand feet from mountains to seashore and, hampered by the depression of a low barometer, fight the enemy as we had fought.

"Mother, that same man's at the door." There he stood with his air of relaxed kindliness. "My wife's cooked dinner," he said. "We want you all to come over – oh, yes, all of you. We've got kids too and know that they can eat." Food! Except to nibble occasionally on a loaf of bread, we had not thought of food since Arthur and I started out so cheerily with our breakfast in the car.

Sarah Ludlam, Joe's wife, stood above the crowd, tall, straight, her hair straight and black, her face browned with forty years of Florida sun, her eyes jubilant. To me she will always typify the spirit above the storm. With water half way to her knees, she had cooked for her family of seven, our family of eight and the family of five next door. "We knew that we all would be a-needin' this stove, so we saved it first." Oh, that dinner! Fried eggs, potatoes, beans and coffee, that big pot of coffee! Our hosts moved among us, unpretentious and eager in their giving, wholesome as the saw palmetto of their Florida fields. "Take money for this dinner? Why sir, we are storm neighbors, this is no time to pay."

We returned to our house, the water was two feet deep in the upstairs rooms. To save what plaster we could, the elder members of the family rolled up skirts and trousers and began to bale. My room was utter dilapidation - the furniture was paintless and the bedstead shot with glass.

"Poor Mr. Hilburn!"

What we did not yet know was that we were saving the house for ourselves – that a stern Florida lease would make us pay for such a wreck.

That night we slept at Arthur's partner's home. His wife Nancy came over with open arms, "Our house is built Georgia fashion, all boards and shingles and close to the ground." I will never dream of marble halls again – leave them to the tourists. Sunday morning, after-a drive through the desecrated city, we returned to our gored windows and soaked trunks in Shenandoah.

Joe Ludlam had lost everything in the storm— the roof of his warehouse and all that was under it. "We must carry each other," Sarah Ludlum spoke quietly. She baked bread for all her neighbors, "there ain't a loaf in town." Afraid of typhoid, we all had to use bottled water, even for the dishes.

Sarah had a sewing machine on her front porch. "Come over, neighbors and sew when you get a breathing spell. The church is a-calling for clothes. Women are sick and dying in the hospitals and the babies are naked. Women, our men need cars and the children need watching, let's do our rescue work right here." This we did. I made gowns and slips between dish washing and drying and cleaning the endless mass of clothes. The burden of apparel! Surely a bathing suit and a pair of pajamas were all any one would ever need again. But worse than the struggle with the clothes was the struggle with the debris about the place. Bushels of grapefruit added to the complexity of unidentified roofing and garbage cans. The heavy sun pressed on us as we worked.

Sarah Ludlam's sewing machine was a real personality. It whirred constantly, accompanied by another sound – the artillery of hammers. The men did not wait a single day to start the roofs. No one had waited – that was the secret of rehabilitation. Sarah had cooked us dinner with her feet in the waters of the Hurricane. Bits of merriment floated about the machine.

"Susie Blake in Coconut Grove tied pillows on the heads of her children to keep the plaster from killing them."

"Three boats came up in our yard. One stuck its head in the kitchen window. It was packed with brooms and coffee. We unloaded her and off she went."

"Why, the water was five feet in our living room. Ma Warren was the only one who couldn't swim so we tied her to the ironing board."

It was on Sarah Ludlam's porch that I heard of tragedies, of reclamation, of the generosity of the outside world.

Sarah and Joe were losing their home. "We can't pay the interest any more, but friends will keep us, storm friends, and things will pick up. When I think of the drowned at Hialeah and Okeechobee, I know that Joe and me ain't no harder hit than we can bear." Only with death is grief. I looked at her face bending above the sewing machine, silhouetted against the quiet sunset. The storm was over. It had left its mark upon us all – upon many the mark of the cross which would linger long into new and more selfish days. Prosperity, even that, could never dim that mark from Sarah Ludlam's soul.

The rattle of the hammers ceased. Sarah smiled and folded her work. A bird called shrilly. "Bless his heart, a catbird. The Hurricane didn't blow that little fellow so far away after all."

Above the Storm

Break the palms and twist the pine-tops From the
    sky.
Split the clouds.
Behold, Jehovah Passes by.

"No, sir," said the man at the filling station, "I ain't
asking you more for gas. This ain't the time to go up on
prices. God knows what happened at the Beach. Them
that tried the Causeway was swept in the Bay, and out
at Hialeah the dead are floating around." "Arthur," I
said, "let's go home. I've seen enough." It was Sunday
morning, the day after the Hurricane - a day of
glittering brightness. We had just driven the entire
length of storm-rent Miami to Arthur's office in the
Buena Vista section. That the tarred roof of the
building lay near us on the ground suddenly did not
seem to matter. There was something sinister behind
this devastation - the one- horror, death.

Slowly we picked our way back through the
storm-shattered city.

Gaunt she lay, naked, torn. Her tall, slender
buildings, emaciated through loss of glass and tile,
reached like palsied fingers toward the sky.

Beneath a clutter, wreckage of land and sea, were
the ruthless lacerations of flood and tempest. But this
time I drove by with unseeing eyes - drove by ships
huddling in the streets, by palms with their haughty
plumes buried in the sand, by ragged holes in concrete
walls from which protruded bathtubs and splintered
bedsteads, look as though the city's mouth had been
pried open to show the cavities in her back teeth; drove
by people who moved noiselessly, saying nothing, their
eyes wide, their hands fluttering over little things -
sweeping the drenched steps of a lopsided house,

hanging muddy garments on an upturned tree, dazedly touching the motley rubbish that once had been a home.

Something to do - their hands must move until they can think themselves through this agony of ruined toys. Only with death is grief. "Out at Hialeah the dead are floating around."

Bones Of The Barracuda

After a quick swim, Eleanor stretched herself on the stone terrace, and, through half shut eyes, watched the curve of ocean, shining like a fallen shield beyond the copper green of her lawn.

She loved to lie like this, unconscious of time, prostrate like the amphibious creatures of the Everglades...

She was roused by piano music drifting through the open windows of the loggia – soft, rambling at first, becoming discontent, strident. She closed her eyes, turned on her side, muffling her ears with her arms, fighting to maintain her mood. It was impossible. The music persisted, creeping like a cold shadow through her senses. Exasperated, she sprang to her feet and entered the house.

Herbert did not look up, although she let the screen door slam behind her. Tensely he bent above the keys of the grand piano, his graying, unkept hair pushed back from his forehead.

Eleanor crossed the patio, circling the fountain of blue water hyacinths. For a moment she stood there, her hand clutching the drapery of the high French window, struggling for self-control.

He played on, regardless, as though she were a shadow. "Herbert, I was trying to rest." His tones grew softer.

"You forget I've been working," her voice was sharp. "Since seven this morning I've been helping Mr. Drew move the spotted crotons – "

"That's what you like." Yawning, he rose to his feet. "Herbert, I can't understand you, you waste your days and resent the fact that I try to accomplish something."

"Must I tell you again? There is nothing here for me to do."

"But you had your music. Why did you let it go to pieces; your chords are pure dissonance. If one of our friends should ask you to play, you're as apt to insult her with your uncanny improvisations."

He walked wearily toward the door, then turned facing her. "This place is a jazz orchestra, a high pitch of unendurable monotony."

Eleanor bit her lip; she could never answer him when he spoke like this. Would he never know the peace she knew in this region of boundless sea and sky, the forgetfulness permeating and sweet as the odor blossoming through April hummocks?

She followed him to the terrace. Before them the sea stretched in a blue flame, the sun flashing rainbows across the almost motionless undulations.

"How wonderful." Eleanor's voice was suddenly gentle, reverent.

For a moment Herbert studied the scene before him, "Yes that's it – wonderful in its monotony – day after day– day after day. Do you know what I've been doing these past twenty years, ever since, like some adventuring troubadour, I came South and married you? I've been swimming one blue wave after another

– first spiritually, then physically, now mentally, till my reason deserts me. It's death, death by slow drowning. Some day, with the white bones of the barracuda, my bones shall be washed ashore. And so will yours, Eleanor." He turned upon her fiercely. "This country will get you yet. Remember, you were not born here. Your Father wrote poetry about flamingoes, but died babbling about mountains and spring freshets."

A dark red surged beneath the tan of Eleanor's face; her eyes glittered.

"Go back to New Hampshire," she cried sharply. "Divorce me if you like– little I care. I can't be happy in your misery. This house is my life; I'll never leave it."

That afternoon Eleanor took her car and drove the Everglades road to Hialeah. She wore a red beach coat and her bare feet were covered by a pair of shapeless slippers. Only in the evenings did she dress. Her days – half garden and half sea - made grooming difficult and obliterated thoughts of personal beauty.

She stopped at Mr. Drew's nursery, a low, earthy house surrounded by swamplike masses of tropical shrubs. She followed the tangled path under a pergola of split palmwood from which hung native air plants of a deep shrimp color, and orchids from Egypt and India, floating like red and purple birds upon nests of twisted fern root. She pushed open the warped door, and in semi-darkness, by means of a flashlight, watched the tropical fish swim in their glass aquariums and moldy cement tanks – guppies, moons, Siamese fighting fish, brilliant as jewels in the cave of Aladdin. Mr. Drew was not there – but that did not matter. She knew that in his quiet way, he welcomed her coming, understanding her joy in the mergence of soul in this mysterious beauty, her inspiration through the sinuous lethe of color.

For an hour she lingered, sitting upon a low stool, transforming sight into sensation, feeling her own body relax into the soft fire of aquatic rhythm.

Darkness fell as she speeded her car down the lonely road skirting the Everglades. The sun now fell, wounded, upon a nest of grass, sending forth, as with a cry, the long shadows of evening, the salty tang of the mangrove swamp.

When she arrived home, Herbert was gone. On the piano lay a note. Her hands trembled as she unfolded the paper. She read –

"I have gone as you suggested. I shall spend two days in Palmwood. If you wish, join me there, otherwise I shall consider our marriage ended. I cannot remain married to the langour of the life you have chosen. Herbert."

Eleanor replaced the note on the piano, and for a moment her eyes swept over the body of the great instrument, gleaming in the gold lamplight. Vaguely she realized that it resembled Herbert, lonely, uncompromising, in the great room, changeless in pattern, dedicated to the soul of great music. That was the trouble. He no longer played Bach or Beethoven, rending the air with the only beauty he seemed to know.

She walked out on the terrace. Moonlight enveloped her. Like fold upon fold of bridal satin, it floated across the night blooming jasmine, walking an odor almost intolerable with sweetness. Eleanor reached out with her arms to the whiteness, shook the light through her blond curles and laughed, suddenly, defiantly. Then getting down upon her knees, she pressed her cheek against the grass.

A few days later, Eleanor walked down to the beach.

She felt like one who has awakened from a long sleep, a sleep which had held Herbert – his unhappiness like a depressing dream through the quiet of her life. She must forget him now, as one forgets the night which is past, the night with its nearness, its yearning, its maladjustment. She must wash away more than twenty years of memories, the bitter ones and those which clung like honey to her lips. For an hour she swam, floated and swam again, tricking the waves with the undulations of her graceful limbs.

With a new feeling of possessiveness, she stepped ashore, crossed the lawn, passed under the group of acacia trees and the long line of royal palms, towering like national monuments beside the driveway. Beneath the striped awning she entered the house. Here everything looked strangely vast and meaningless – the dark paneling, the heavy furniture of intricately carved oak. But it was only the piano which made her think of Herbert – the piano and a picture of the mangrove swamp – short trees with great roots wrapping themselves like snakes across the canvas. As she walked, her feet made bright spots on the red tile.

"Cora," she asked, entering the kitchen, "what have we for dinner?"

Cora looked up slowly, her face an expressionless piece of black mahogany. She was peeling an avocado, and the green rind, graceful as a grass snake, fell upon the white table.

"There's plenty," her voice was low, vaguely rebellious. "You remember the papaya, then there's the chicken we baked." Eleanor's mind worked quickly, here eyes following the curves of the avocado.

"I'm going to town, Cora, and I shall bring home some guests – two, maybe three. I'll stop at the market and buy some stone crab and a cake. You can make some ice cream from the mango. Will you be ready?"

Cora's hand placed the avocado on the table, slowly as in deep thought.

"What's the matter?" Eleanor spoke crossly, "the work's half done."

Cora's mouth grew stubborn. "They say a hurricane's commin', Miss Eleanor I'm goin' home."

"Hurricane, ridiculous! There are never hurricanes here – only big blows. But if you are nervous, you may stack the dishes after and I'll drive you home. That's fair, isn't it?"

"Yes, ma'am," Cora didn't look up.

Eleanor tripped out her feet, soft thuds on the blue linoleum.

An hour later, in a pleated chiffon dress and a white straw hat, she started her car down the driveway. Her heart beat gaily, happily and there was a tingle of adventure in her veins. The air was cooler and a light, but steady wind was blowing. She thought of Cora. How superstitious she was! It was almost night when she returned – alone. She ran to the house, swept forward by the driving wind and rain.

"Cora," she called, "here help me shut this door.

Cora!" Finally she closed the door, pressing it with her whole body. She turned the great key and fled into the kitchen – it was empty. On the table, like an evil eye, gleamed the avocado.

For hours, alone, with only a flashlight against the darkness, Eleanor fought the storm. She tried to light the candles, cupping the flames with her hands, they would flare and disappear. She heard the telephone pole crash; the awnings rip from their steel frames and fling themselves like battering rams against the glass windows; she watched the mad water pour down the stairs; felt the house tremble as with ague, and the wild unison of wind and rain shriek with the continuous agony of a factory whistle. Hours passed. Her keen terror subsided into mentle dullness, and physical indifference. She pulled some cushions on top of a lounge, in a far corner where the water did not come, and fell asleep.

The pale light of morning shone through the windows when she awoke. The silence was heavy, steamy like marsh fog. Was this the lull, or was the storm over? Eleanor had heard of hurricanes with their hot treachery of lulls, but she could not remember – not exactly. Anyway, everything seemed safe enough now. She would take the car and drive about – too bad if anyone were hurt.

She walked out.The big awning sprawled across the front steps, two palms lay with their heads crushed upon the driveway. "They can be replanted," she thought, "and the upstairs window can be replaced." She got into her car and slowly backed from the garage. "The lawn's like a pond but I can make it. It only takes..."The words were swept from her mouth. For with a hiss the sleeping hurricane awoke, uncurled and struck with deadly fangs straight from the ocean. With the fury of escaping steam – no stops, no diminuendoes, about her in ruthless massacre, once more wind and rain, and this time ocean ruled the earth.

On all sides trees went over.The tar roof from the

garage avalanched to the road; tile showered through the gray, engulfing the mess.

Eleanor could not hold the car. The brakes had needed relining for a long time. It had not seemed to matter much – such flat roads, and she always drove slowly, but no... Back, back she went before the horror of the invisible wind, the gun shot power of the rain. Or were these waves, lashing in thin whips against her windshield. She pulled upon the brakes till her hands ached, prayed, shouted for help, screamed as she felt the crash.

When she opened her eyes, she was alone, lying in her living room upon the grand piano. Light glittered through the shattered windows of the sunroom; wreckage littered the floor; gaunt holes stared at her from the once plastered walls. Not far away floated the painting of the mangrove swamp.

How still everything seemed, breathless, waiting, the approach of some new terror. Loneliness swept over Eleanor, loneliness which she had never known through the long bright days of the past – loneliness for the house which had betrayed her, which leered at her like a friend gone mad – loneliness for Herbert she had hidden from herself, and for the imperfect realization of her marriage. Herbert – here she lay on his piano. His because on these strings, he had strummed his protest, beaten his soul. She could almost see his face, looking at her above the keys, white with misery. Where was he now? Why was she lying in this ravished house? Could she ever live in it again, build it from the wreckage, feel its lure enfold her? Could she ever move again in the haze of forgetfulness, the perfume of flowers, the enchantment of shining days, of nights heavy with moon or stars?

Hot tears stung her cheeks. She tried to move. Terrible pain shot through her knee. She looked and saw her leg bound with a man's shirt. She groaned and lay still; it seemed no use to try. Someone had been kind, whoever it was would return. The throb in her knee grew worse. She thought of her father bound to his chair. Long ago he had come, had bought this house, seeking for peace. He had not found it. He had died calling for the hills.

Had she stifled her life as he had stifled his, giving her soul utterly to sensation, watching a house ruin her husband and not care?

When she heard footsteps coming toward her through the water, she closed her eyes. It seemed natural that someone should come – someone or death. She knew that it must be Mr. Drew. He, of all the world, would be eager to bind up her wounds as he would bind up the broken plants. But for her everything had changed. The curtain had fallen upon the brilliant comedy of her days, and Mr. Drew was part of that comedy – the sincere part which brings tears to the eyes of the spectators even while they laugh.

"Are you hurt much, Miss?" His voice was kind, pitying as one speaks to a child.

"I suppose so."

"I'm sorry I had to go, but there are so many others." "Tell me." "Out in Hialea, the dead are floating around." Eleanor quivered as from a lash. Death - something else to hold her. "God," she groaned, "save me."

"Yes Miss." He did not understand.

"Take me to the depot, Mr. Drew. I must leave town today – at once."

"There are no trains – tracks all littered up." "Then drive me to Palmwood. I'll pay you fifty dollars, anything you ask."

"I don't know – maybe we can make it somehow. But lady, you're hurt."

"Yes, but there's a hospital in Palmwood. Take me there. What time is it?"

"About three o'clock."

"We can get there before night if you hurry. Help me, and God bless you."

"My car is here. Maybe the Everglades Road will be best." He looked about uneasily. "Isn't there something you want?"

"Only my purse. It was in the car with me." He put it in her hand.

Eleanor opened her eyes and smiled faintly. "If I cry don't mind – only drive."

The sky spread blue peaceful, as though forgetting in it the wild onslaught of wind and water.The road stretched through wastes. Eleanor, lying as best she could on the back seat, did not see what had happened.The agony of her knees, the tragedy of others, nothing must hold her now. Only cowards flee at such a time as this, she thought. Yet Cora ran from the hurricane. "She was right to desert me for her little children at home. Now I must desert my house, my neighbors and go to my husband. He is not in Palmwood," she thought, "he has gone on, I too must go on, later when I'm well."

"To the hills, father loved the hills – I only remember the cold. But its not my happiness that I'm seeking, but forgiveness."

The hospital at Palmwood was a white, rambling building overlooking the water. The nurses were kind, and after a while Eleanor's knees knit and she could walk. She wrote to Herbert, praying that he encourage her to continue the pilgrimage she had begun. His note of sympathy was short, impersonal. "You have had a great shock. Winters up north are dangerous to those accustomed to constant sun. I'm sorry about your knee."

"Shall I go on?" She questioned herself. "Am I surgeon enough to heal the wound I have made?"

Mr. Drew wrote, "My heart aches over your poor place. Come back and let me help you before it is utter ruin.

"I am only half way on my journey," thought Eleanor. "If Herbert needed me, it would be easy to go on. The house needs me, but I dare not return." She walked up and down the hospital porch. The sun sparkled on the ocean before her – pricks of fire through the soft swell of cobalt blue. "I will wade out and let the sea quiet me," she thought. "He had always solved my problems, like a kind of great father. Only once was his chastisement more than I could bear." She put on a bathing suit, and almost happily tripped down to the sand; just in time to meet the long, white, lazy curve of an incoming wave.

On and on she went – swimming and resting, swimming and resting again. "I will go on till the ocean tells me," she thought. "I am too weak to make decisions – I need strength." But something was happening to her knee – pain, sudden, terrible pain that had come the day she had opened her eyes upon the piano, and had looked into the dismal decaying cavities of her home.

But something else was happening, something more powerful than man or human suffering, something relentless as the will of God – the tide was going out, "Out in Hialeah the dead are floating around." Eleanor knew that the little strength that was hers, the strength for which she had prayed had become one with the great ocean. She was his as the other dead were his. With them she was one of the happy unfortunates – happy because there were no more decisions to make, unfortunate because death seems not as beautiful as the color of earth and sky, hibiscus and palm, or lips if one should love. Eleanor understood it all so much better now. She had been put on probation for a little while, that was all. Her knee had been fractured in the great storm and not her skull. She had been given two months in which to regain her womanhood, two months in which to disentangle her soul from the roots of the mangrove, the scent of the bay bloom in April – but she had remained the same, she had not yearned as much for her husband, her son, as to feel beneath her fingers the tremulous black and gray of her garden. And so she too was one of the victims. The struggle which had come between, was but a dream. Today the ocean did not scurge the earth, digging caverns in the sand. But serene and gentle he rocked his children on his breast, murmuring through the swell and flow of waters the peace of sleep.

Atlanta: 1933

When Kate finally wearied of endless sun, and Arthur tired of his law practice in Florida, the family returned to Atlanta. They purchased a house which had been owned by a MacLeod cousin of Kate's. It became the home for all the children and grandchildren, just as Mountain Hall had been for the generation before. The family christened it Cane Brake, often shortened to Canebrake.

Cane Brake

Stalks of the bamboo tatter
The sky to flickering leaves -
Free
As the rock of the wind
In a sail of "The Golden Hind"
Their fragments found
From scrolls of ancient China
To snows of Fuji-yama.

Gracious, a cane brake refuses
To battle, so bows
Low, while the hurricane passes;
Then rising in scorn
(Too majestic for probe)
He restles the silk
Of his Mandarin robe.

April Thoughts, 1966

My own musings and memories about the house: Canebrake is an old house, big and magic. Compared to other places, it is neither old nor big, just one of many houses in one of Altanta's older heighborhoods, Ainsley Park, but to Codington grandchildren, it seemed mysteriously old and infinitely big, just the same. The scope of the house extended out the doors and windows, past the wide porches and into the yard.

Fairies and elves lived near this house, but not inside because they preferred the flowers and bamboo. Their magic rested in the house with the people who lived there, and touched all who visited, especially those who had the privilege of staying a while.

Upon approaching the house, the first thing you saw was the front yard, covered with English ivy, interspersed with daffodils, and lorded over by a row of blooming azaleas. The yard was free to all growing things. Kate was an indifferent gardener who insisted that 'nature knows no weeds.' She let even the most stubborn invaders have a season.

The front porch stretched from the driveway at the right of the big green house, past the porch-swing and rocking chairs, where it turned round the corner past the living room windows, ending in a screened spot with a door to the dining room.

If you knew where they were hiding, just below the porch, there were child-size houses and hiding places for dolls, and if your eyes looked forward and traveled skyward, you would see the cane, the house's namesake, shimmering in the Atlanta light, and if your eyes stayed on that cane for a minute longer than an adult should, the fairies and elves might make themselves visible.

The front door of Canebrake was guarded by pots of hopeful geraniums and a crepe myrtle tree, gnarled and twisted. It was perfect for climbing and catching small feet.

All the downstairs connected to the front hall. The "date room," a small parlor to the right of the foyer, was used by the Codington girls for entertaining their young men, and later became a den and junk room for scrabble boards and old golf clubs. No matter its use, it never lost its name. Next came the living room, set backwards, to the left of the front door. It was defined by its faded rose couch, glassed lawyers' bookshelves, and Arthur's staring dragon chair - an unusual throne with dragon arms and pearl eyes. It had been given to him by a grateful client.

On the other side the living room was the dining room, the largest, and most important room inside Canebrake. The dining room opened back to the front hall, and connected it to the living room and the kitchen. Here, dining was not only for people. Birds were fed at the window, next to the heavy oak table. A large chest, its drawers full of silver and childhood wonders such as bottles of bugle beads, tin soldiers and pink dancing dolls, stood next to the old black piano, at the door to the kitchen.

The kitchen, a crowded room, was sort of an afterthought. Its shelves were overloaded with dishes, cereal boxes and cat food. The walls were dark green, and the white steel table in the center of the room was always covered with fresh fruits and vegetables.

Behind the kitchen door was the back porch. A dilapidated ironing board and a ping-pong table were its only furniture. Out the old door and down a few steps to the back yard, there was another world. A fig tree was planted to the left of the steps, as near the house as was practical. Kate bought the tree with the five dollars she had won from a poetry contest. She felt she was better able to reward her winning with a tree rather than lunch. She relished beating her spoiled birds to the figs.

The rest of the backyard was still and jungle-like, kudzu covering the trees at the far back at the border with the train tracks, and day lilies blooming orange along the edges of the yard.

Canebrake was a house of children and fairytales, a yard of birds, squirrels and hiding in the cane. We never saw it as untamed, a yard which Jasper, my grandmother's gardener might despair, but rather it was a wonderland, glorious overgrown chaos, especially to us northern grandchildren, a place of beauty and joy. A cousin once remarked; "you could take me all around the world blindfolded, but if you brought me back here, I'd know immediately that I was back at Canebrake, that I was home."

Nature

As with everything else in her life, Kate's religiosity was joyous. She wove that joy into all aspects of her life. She attended the Episcopal Church and had a deep sense of Christianity, but her beliefs were more broad than was common. Rather than believing in one God as far away as Heaven, her God was everywhere, in each droplet of water and blade of grass. Like the Civil War generation that raised her, she despised killing, especially in mechanized war, and although both her parents were hunters and taxidermists, Kate could not condone the unnecessary killing of animals or the clear-cutting of forests. A keen observer of life, she noted the good and the mistakes she saw around her. She was not afraid to gently stop an overwrought mother from hitting her child, or chiding her readers to take better care of their world.

Here are a few examples from her newspaper column, which like most of her poems, celebrate the natural world in a deeply spiritual way. I have included one of the later ones which, I believe best reflect the theme of newspaper columns written fifty years earlier.

Birds and Golf

The hunting season has opened. Once more we hear the happy bark of the pointer and see the flash of newly polished shotguns. Over our Georgia fields they tramp, these tired businessmen, donned in boots and khaki, following the over- grown trail, the lure of the tangled and unfrequented wilds. Out they go, clothed in their regained freedom, stretching themselves to the tune of Nature, out on the first vocation of man - The Chase.

And we who love the birds, the feathered creatures of our woods, who mourn over the disappearance of the wild pigeon, the past record of slaughtered doves, who, in spite of present restricted game laws, find poor comfort during the months that these laws are suspended, what are we to do?

Have you ever watched a covey of partridges from the time when, egg-shells kicked aside, each youngster scampered out into the open behind the old quail mother, till the time when this family of a dozen bold Bob Whites gave forth their whistles to the wind? If so, you can understand the "Audubon Society" the "Bird Lovers" the women who refuse to wear aigrettes and, real bird wings upon their hats.

Jane Addams has demonstrated at Hull House that a wise direction, rather than a curbing of native instinct and energy, works for the greatest good. Our birds already have protection, and that protection is growing from year to year in Athletic Sports. The wild ducks on their southern flight might be surprised to know that the gymnasium, football, baseball and the golf links are doing more for their conservation than public sentiment and game laws combined. Our boys must grow. They demand the spirit of competition with their fellows in physical prowess, in the spirit of the game, which is the spirit of The Chase.

Over the golf links the birds fly peacefully. And as habits of life make habits of thought, so the sportsman is learning to appreciate birds for their charm and usefulness apart from their value as food and the excitement of killing. Our attitude toward life makes life what it is, and it is our attitude toward the birds which will finally save them.

Macon Daily Telegraph, Dec. 5, 1915

Fur Trimmings

This winter the extravagant use of furs in the trimming of hats, suits and gowns has caused an enormous and needless waste of animal life. We may seek to justify the wearing of skins for protection from the cold, but women should refuse to countenance styles which sacrifice blood for mere personal adornment.

Macon Daily Telegraph, Jan. 9, 1916

Gasoline

It is six o'clock, cold and raining, but the down-town street is ablaze with light. The light streams not only from the flarey globes of the great white ways, and the zig - zag whirl of electric signs, but from the thousand fiery eyes of automobiles and motor trucks crowded and jammed upon the narrowed pavement.

Where are the horses which a few years ago shivered in this spot, unblanketed on a night such as this? Could we call them back from the bloody battlefields of Europe, or from the shadowy unknown fast enshrouding the passing of these magnificent animals? Would we be more humane, more compassionate, we whose allegiance is sworn so fully, so absolutely to the KING of GASOLINE.

Macon Daily Telegraph, Nov. 19, 1916

Trash

The leaves are falling, crisp, brown, light as curled
wafers, seeking the cool heart of Earth, fulfilling the
silent plan of Nature to renew the weary soil.
    Quickly we brush them into heaps, burn them, and
call them trash.

Macon Daily Telegraph, Nov. 19, 1916

The Last March

The trees, departing,
Bore their shadow with them -
Reflections gentian-amber,
From the still water.
And their going was the sound
Of ax and saw,
And the whimper
Of evicted wind.

But who will follow the torn
Path of the refugees,
Or, in ritual
Of pyre or burial,
Gather their naked fragments?
And who will ease to green oblivion
A bandage round the lake? That pale myopic eye,
Blinking in painful tears
Beneath the sun.

Shod With Light, 1966

It was a delight to walk through the woods among the great, noble hardwood trees of Atlanta, which she described once as "fountains, springing upward and falling back in myriad droplets of leaf," The smallest star shaped flower did not escape her notice or her tenderness. She observed every curve of bough, every ripening of blackberry or persimmon. There was no living thing in the woods that she did not greet with happy recognition, calling each by name. When a common pokeberry plant suddenly appeared in a stone box of petunias on the front porch, she was not disdainful of its taking up residence on exclusive property, but was filled with admiration for the impudent courage it had shown. She nearly wept on the day she discovered that some well-meaning hand had twisted the pokeberry's tough purple stem and all but uprooted it. Only careful replanting, daily watering, and at last seeing the pokeberry's purple fruit lording it over the petunias brought her comfort.

Catherine Shafer, personal Correspondence, 1979.

Atlanta

In 1952 Arthur compiled his poems in Jest about Georgia, a book of limericks, each about a different Georgia city.

WHY OUR CAPITAL GROWS

Great loaves from little yeast cakes grow:
First "The Standing Peach Tree" -
Soon a million
or so
Now the Dogwood City
Needs only a ditty
To tell why it rises - we knead the dough.

Jest About Georgia, 1952

The Ainsley Park section of Atlanta, where the Codingtons made their home, is marked with long curving roads designed to resemble parkways instead of suburban blocks. The roads succeed in giving the residential area the feeling of countryside, rather than a community mere minutes from downtown Atlanta. This feeling is nearly as true today as it was when the Codingtons moved into their house on Avery Drive in 1933. Always involved with her children's lives, Kate wrote this story around 1935. Her two youngest girls were about thirteen and eleven at that time.

Dog House

Behind the creation of most buildings stands a personality, but behind the summer house in McClatchey Park, in the Ainsley Park section of Atlanta, lies the story of a dog.

More than ten years ago, at a veterinarian hospital, Lawrence Tibbett, a plump gold and white collie, died of a heart attack. Up to this time he had been a great favorite in the neighborhood, and because of his beauty and affable disposition, each summer his young master had entered him in the pet show. And what shows these were - dogs, cats, lizards, frogs, birds. Every creature that walked, crawled, or flew was eligible. Upon this yearly occasion, and under the admiring eyes of the owners, many queer specimens were herded to the playground.

For several consecutive seasons, Tibbitt had won a blue ribbon; first for being "Biggest Dog," the next year for being, "Prettiest Dog," and the last - well that was the year of the big thunder storm.

On that fatal afternoon the crowd of children and animals attending the pet show was unusually large. It was midsummer, and the little girls were colorful in fresh organdies, and the little boys in Sunday shorts. Suddenly, and without warning, lightning ripped through an unnoticed cloud, and in less time than it takes to say "Jack Robinson," the rain simply plunged. With squeals, hugging or dragging their pets, the youngsters fled into a nearby house.

After a few moments of head-over-heels scrambling for standing place in the crowded living room, there were a few seconds of quiet, but only a few. For Tibbett, his dander aroused by the turn of events, espied against the opposite wall the large white, wooly dog that a few minutes before had been his rival in the "beauty contest." Without even the challenge of a yelp, he leaped the distance between himself and his opponent. The fight was instant and terrific, the worst fight that ever happened in a living room. Pandemonium was complete: children, pets, tables, chairs swam in a huddle of unearthly racket. Somehow, one of the mothers, and ex-officio owner of the white angel, managed to disentangle him from the jaws of Tibbett and drag him to her car.

Peace was won. But the show was ruined, and it was a woebegone group of young Atlantans that wended its way homeward under the clearing skies. And, if I remember correctly, Tibbett walked with his tail high. After all, was he not the victor? But here the real story begins.

The next morning, five determined little girls, headed by two adverturous teenagers, called on the Mayor at the County Court House. They were admitted with a smile. What happened after this we learned from the morning newspaper, where a picture of the group decorated the front page. These delegates presented their case to the Mayor and the assembled officials. And to make their plea more colorful, they sang "My Country 'Tis of Thee." In this wonderful interview, the Mayor learned that McClatchey Park was headquarters for health, fun and civic pride. But what, oh what was the use in the face of a thunderstorm?

Well, it was all a howling success! And with the sanction of the Mayor, the generous city of Atlanta donated several thousand dollars for the building of a 'summer house' in McClatchey Park.

Look at it when you pass— sexangular in shape, built of Georgia granite and pine, and with a pagoda-styled roof of red tile. There is even a tiny basement, equipped with a gas heater, where Mrs. Johnson, the supervisor, can warm her feet on frosty mornings. And everything happens here: birthday parties, checker games, but best of all it is "a refuge in time of storm."

But to those of us who remember, and love to

remember, call this "Tibbett's House." For after all it was built because of a dog.

Philosophy and War

Kate had a strong sense of justice, a deep moral base. During the time she was writing her column in the Macon Daily Telegraph, the First World War began in Europe. It became obvious that America was going to become involved. Kate had a deep hatred of war, a feeling that war was never worth the death and waste. She had learned this, almost inherited it, from her father, who was in the regiment that preceded Sherman's march through South Carolina, and from her aunts, his sisters, who had born the brunt of nursing the returning soldiers. Their stories of worry and outright fear as the Union troops marched into their city, the capital, quartered in their neighborhood, stealing their food and silver, stayed with Kate.

Kate wrote poems and stories expressing her pacifism, her sadness and fears for the soldiers, their families, and the nation as it prepared to enter the World War. She opposed the United States becoming involved in the European war, and although this was a feeling shared by many at the time, the newspaper editors admonished her to keep her pacifism out of her columns. She refused, and they dismissed her, ending the weekly column. Here are a few of the poems that were published, some that were not, and some later works on the subject of war.

The Dead Recruit

They paint a halo round you, shattered Boy
Out where the sands lie waste beneath the rain
Or is it blood that drops so ceaselessly
Upon your eyes dim-horrored to the pain?
They paint a halo where the great shell burst,
Tearing the soul from out your soldier breast
Or was your heart a child's lone heart that yearned

For home and rest?
They paint a halo where your bannered youth,
High-flung to greet the crowding, eager years,
Lies crushed as crumpled flowers at your feet
Or wreath of funeral tears.
They paint a halo...
Do you see it, Boy,
The hero splendor and the glory deed,
The bow far-spanned to golden urns of fame
Or see you murdered as the
Vultures feed?

Macon Daily Telegraph, Nov. 25, 1915

Mothers of War

Whence come all of the men
That throttle the earth with hate?
Why Mothers forged their sons of steel
To rivet the ribs of State.
Whence come all of the dead
That rot on the mangled plain?
Why Mothers gave them as sacrifice

To rulers drunk with slain.
Whence comes all of the blood,
Smirched red on the sodden snow?
Why Mothers fed it out of their hearts
To babies long ago.

Unpublished, 1915

The Game

God laughs at death
Knowing the dead
Forever seek his face -
Drawn upward like the mist beneath the sun -
While moments run.
And years and centuries.
"And who are you," He questions,
"You and You?
"And where the place?
"And was it pestilence,
"Or reckless fun?
"Or age and loneliness
"Demanding rest
"Beneath the green embellishment of grass?
"But hark, new zest
"New rush of feet
"Crowding to pass!
"Children, so quick you come!
"What game below? What noise?"

"We play at war, kind Father,"
Shy they speak,
"You hear the toys."

Shod With Light, 1966

To A Military Cemetery

Move on, move on, white crosses on the hill.
Make way - The dead arise,
Stampede from darkness, rend the earth, and
    stand
In fury and surprise.
Where are the years - the young abandoned years,

The peace, the brotherhood, the goal desired?
Where is the glory, love, and heritage,
The child they might have sired?

Move on, dull stones.
Rebellion of the slain
Shall crash the sanctity of blood and woe.
Retreat.
The Christ you symbolize and shame
Struggles below.

Shod With Light, 1966

Big Guns

Big gun in the market,
Big gun on the hill...
Feed his mouth with silence;
Hold his muzzle still.
Mosses climb the doorstep,
Mosses creep the tomb...
Time erases slowly

Ravages of doom.
Big gun of the spirit,
Big gun of the heart...
And every bullet aimed at God
When the bullets start.

Shod With Light, 1966

Again Thermopylea

Oh was it you or I
Or just an hour-glass
That turned the warring legions
From the Pass?
For bluettes down the valley-lands are blowing
And fig and grape about the cottage growing
And farmer sowing.

Oh was it missile, bomb,
Heroics or the trust
Of man in man that smote
The swords with rust?

Ark of the Everglades, 1975

During the Joseph McCarthy era, when our country stood on the brink of becoming a police state, I was working as a research scientist with the Federal Government. I was young, idealistic and militant. I was opposed to McCarthyism and I espoused a world federation idea, in foreign affairs; an idea of international cooperation, even with the Russians.

Needless to say, my ideas were looked upon with disfavor by the Federal Agency under which I worked. Finally, I was handed a letter charging me with being "disloyal to the Government of the United States of America." I still consider this action against me and against thousands of others courageous enough to oppose the autocratic policies in domestic affairs, and the cold war in foreign affairs, to be a period of great infamy in our nation's history. In any case, I told my mother of this development. She expressed no surprise, and showed no disappointment that her son had gotten himself into trouble. Instead, she turned to me and said,

"John I think it's fine that you have these ideas, but I think you are a fool for getting caught."

Memoir of John F. Codington, 1979

John used his dismissal from the National Institute of Health as an opportunity to move abroad and work in Paris, France. He spent two years there. These were the years just after World War II, and he was horrified at the destruction, and frightened of what humanity was capable of destroying. He toured Europe by train and bicycle, feeling hopeful of a new world that might be created from the ruins of the old, but he was often shocked and overtaken with feelings of despair as the reality of Europe's recent history invaded his thoughts. He wrote his mother asking her to help him understand how humanity could so lose its way. He asked how it was that he was never warned or forced to understand man's cruelty. Kate's reply follows.

Letter to John in France: 1948 or 1949.
Wednesday

I will go back some years. For, as you say, our
environment shapes our characters, rather it tints the
glasses through which we must look at life.

I was brought up in a family of ideals. Although
there was no specific goal, the motives of life were
never allowed to become tawdry or greedy. I, with my
brothers and sisters, still live in the spiritual era which
existed before the Civil War. Broad - modern, yes, all
that, but our glasses are colored and the toad beside the
road is a cardinal with crimson wings. Singing, we
continue our way and because we have seen this beauty
we find rest in spite of a sometime empty pocketbook
or crying baby.

During the First World War I was never partisan. I
wept over all soldiers, all mothers. Pity, that was my
emotion, exhaustless pity and love. After the armistice
when the world went wild, I excused it, blaming the
war as the contaminator, insisting on man's
fundamental innocence.

Personally my life was sheltered from drunkenness
and other debauchery. When evils came my way, I felt
it was up to me to destroy them, but the rosy colors of
my glasses continued to deceive. I passed on unhurt
and unseeing except the beauty which burned me with
the exaltation of the poet. The present war, (World
War II), has been maturing. Because this maturity
comes late, after a life of human affection and
gentleness, it shall not cause me to become bitter or
hopeless.

Now I see man, the good man, as a complex
creature, who through ruthlessness saved and

developed his body in a dangerous world. His spiritual life is new and lacks the emotions of his original sin. It is like the flames upon the altar beneath whose stones are the corruptions of death.

Thank God, this does not make the flames less real, and their power to spread is indeed that of fire. But the wind may come, such as this war. The flames flicker perilously near to extinction. But the rottenness beneath remains — it is there. Unless reborn into the spirit of Christ, as you see it, all men are more or less stained with depravity. Under certain conditions they could watch their enemy hung and gloat.

Now back to your personal problem. Neither Poppy or I prepared you sufficiently to meet the evil of the world. This was first through ignorance. For although Poppy is a man and comes in touch with much wickedness, aesthetically vice to him is most repulsive. He prefers to wear rose glasses. As for me, the only way I knew in which to meet life was individually to sustain ideals and Christianity. What could I tell you beyond this? A child in evil surroundings sees them, avoids them but is not necessarily contaminated. The child of a drunkard is often wonderful.

In some ways you have just left home, for Emory and Charlottesville surrounded you with the type of idealism which was stronger than the surrounding sinfulness. Now as a man of twenty-five, with clear eyes and without the adjustments of the drunkard's son, you see the picture, and at the worst time of all times of the history of the world. It's bad, but don't let it distress you too much. It will not get you; it must not make you unhappy. There is so much beauty in the toughest person. Think of it as fire, how little fuel will make that beauty glow.

We must console ourselves with that. Brother William says that more than anything he regrets the gentleness with which he was brought up. "Why didn't they throw things at me," he said, "and make me tough?" Yes and no. All that is really worthwhile in his character might have been lost, one more hard man, do we need him?

And so, it's best not to blame too much on our bringing up, if it were done in all sincerity. I don't. In the end, my illusions may prove to be the most worthwhile of my experiences. Certainly experience with evil is a slow and painful school. It ends in this, we must be brave and sustain our sense of proportion. Neither should we chastise ourselves eternally as to whether or not we are following the right course. Of course it is the right course if the spirit behind it is genuine. Dr. Mosely tells the story of a washer woman who served Christ as a real Christian by singing "Jesus Loves Me," in time to her scrubbing. "Not what we do, but how we do it." "Not what we believe, but how we believe it." Many a young man had turned to the ministry and had the beartbreak of talking to empty pews, thinking that that way was the only way to serve Christ. It's not the only way. Your talents are the only permanent way, everything else is writing upon water. Do your daily chore, love it, love the man who works with you. The glory of God is about you, though your workshop be a prison cell. Do you remember the poem about the Monk and the angel? The angel visited the monk in his cell. The bell tolled, time for the monk to go to the chapel. Finally he left his celestial guest and spent the hour as was his custom. When he returned he found the angel still there, and the angel said, "If thou hadst staid, I must have fled." God is in your hands -

chemistry. New life, the future, new health, new understanding for the future. Let not the evil of the world disturb! It will cave in, suddenly, unexpectedly. You have a sword, use it, sanely, quietly. Some day the walls of Jericho will fall. We believe this; we believe in the possibilities of men. Now to heal our souls of worry, that is the last enemy and the worst.

A heart full of love-
Mother.

Women: Mothers and Daughters

American women won the right to vote in 1920. Though Kate was never a radical in any way, her belief in "right" was powerful. As with education, she believed that women would succeed if they had the right tools, and were respected. I do not know if this poem was ever published, it is followed by letters to the Macon Daily Telegraph's editor about women.

Woman To Man

I have lived as you bade me live.
Throughout the years I have sunnied your
    moments with smiles,
And dewed them with tears.
For you I have mended and tended;
Have succored and fed;

Have borne the anguish of children;
And buried the dead.
I have followed the trail of the hunter,
To cook your game;
Clambered the ramparts of battle,
To blazon your fame;
Stilled the pain of my yearning
From age to age;
And stifled the prayer that demanded
My heritage.

But now that thought has grown
With a broader day,
Science is tilling the fields
And mowing the hay,
I turn again to the past,
And see it anew
And behold, through the intricate whole,
But the pattern of you!
I look down the dust of the journey,
For centuries back,

And find that my foot-print is ever
Enclosed in your track.
I see where the way has been crooked
That might have been straight;
I feel that my will should be stayed you,
But slumbered too late.
And I know now that shoulder to shoulder,
Everywhere,
My thought, free and vital with your thought,
Should do and should dare;
Should fathom the wealth and the secret
Of earth and of sky,

The need that is biggest and fiercest,
The weaklings cry.
As you wield forth the power of being,
I too would arise,
A-steel with the arm of my purpose,
The truth of my eyes;
While I blaze forth a trail for my children
From vice and from war
While I give them the wings of my courage,
The shield of my law.
So onward, as you would mount onward,
Never to cease,
Unfurling the stars of my heaven
In banners of peace,
I would fling out the lamps of their beauty
As flags, where the feet
Of manhood and womanhood, equals,
In liberty meet.

Unpublished, 1916

WOMAN' RIGHT TO VOTE

To the Editor Macon News:
The question is, what has she the right to do? The mother, has she not the right to vote? What though she may be slow, from force of tradition and habit. She who loves most knows best the needs of childhood. Give her opportunity to follow the six year old fledgling to the schoolhouse door, and education will be enriched. Put her in a position better to guard her boys and girls from the lure of temptation, and the "social problem" will approach its solution. Should not the working girl vote, thus aiding in the struggle for shorter hours and better pay? Has not the woman with

property the right to vote, and thereby protect her own? But what of the rest of womankind? Are they all indifferent, illiterate, or criminal? Are we more afraid to take chances with their vote than on the thousands of immigrants and unestablished men?

What man will throw at woman the first stone? Who thus will assume himself woman's superior? Not superior? Morally, only a more capable and useful citizen in all else that counts. Who is so sure of his own wisdom and judgment, of his patriotism and purpose that he can say to women, "We have no need of you, outside your home your ideas and help are blank and unprofitable."

But it is said that women have indirect influence, influence upon their husbands, sons and friends. What a poor makeshift is this, cultivating as it does the spirit of "lobbying" and a personal exploitation of feminine wiles.

It is refreshing to know that some men have their own opinions, and need neither masculine nor feminine advice. Besides, is indirect influence effective? The women of Massachusetts worked forty years for a measure which the women of Colorado obtained in one year.

And you men, who do not vote except as an afterthought, how can you accuse your sisters of indifference? Rather help them to grow, as they will help you. Broaden out together in ideals of real citizenship. Realize that rights cannot be "cornered," but are God-given equally to woman as to man. Look upon the duty of the ballot as a privilege for service. Call for more efficiency, if you will, purer motive, better mind. However you may limit the suffrage, you have no right to limit it on account of sex.

Letter to editor, Macon Daily News, 1918

HEIMATH HALL - FOR WOMEN

It has taken centuries to develop women's appreciation of their vital relation to each other which now, expressed through the modern women's movement, is sweeping a glorious wave of sisterhood upon the shores of humility.

The women of Macon were not the last to respond to this call. In fact they caught the keynote of conditions by realizing that one of the pivots of this new order is the working girl. They saw that the wage-earning woman has come to stay, and that upon her character as well as that of the homemaker, the fabric of our nation rests. They understood, too, that working girls are paid little, that to keep their self-respect and place as citizens they must have a living wage.

To make this ideal possible, Heimath Hall was established. Here working girls could live, protected by the sacred rights of home, and allowed to save from their means enough to dress decently and to meet the common obligations of life.

This was Heimath Hall of the past. Heimath Hall of the future possesses a broader ideal than this. Not deserting her old standards, she is planning to maintain in her new $30,000 building fifty girls. She expects to throw open her doors to the women of Macon. She is to be a modern YWCA without its limitations. Someone has said that the South's greatest problem is its frail women. Heimath Hall is to solve this problem here by possessing an up to date swimming pool and gymnasium. Besides this, there is to be an assembly hall for women's meetings, a room for the business women's Bible class, rest rooms, etc. And over all is to be thrown an atmosphere conducive to the development and growth of pure, strong womanhood.

There is a call for help. You men who enjoy the YMCA, think a moment. Has not woman's love, work and interest helped to build this for you? The time has come when that which is best in women ask your aid. Help your sisters to gain the independence, which is worth far more than fine clothes or jewelry. Do not scorn their demands nor criticize the necessity which forces them to come to you for assistance. We are all dependent upon each other, and we are equally responsible for race betterment. Give something to Heimath Hall. Out of ancient jealousies and petty envying, there shines no more beautiful light on earth than that which gleams from the slogan of the cause fronting you now, "Women for women."

Letter to editor,Macon Daily Telegraph 1917

Writing

As the six children neared adulthood, married and moved out of the house, Kate found more time for writing and music. She had taught piano for many years but now she had time for real practicing and more pupils. She joined the Atlanta Writer's Club, which she chaired in the early fifties, The National League of American Penwoman, Inc., The Georgia Writers Association, and a group called the Every Saturday Club.

Emily Hightower remembered the Every Saturday Club which she and Kate, and other neighbors attended.

The Every Saturday Club, which usually met twice a month, (and never on Saturday), was a research and discussion group. Members chose an overall topic about once a year, and individuals wrote and presented papers on specific topics within that theme. Aunt Kate was always so well prepared. She would sit there with her notes on her lap, so ladylike, so sweet. And she'd present her paper. She would never look at her notes.There they'd be just sitting in her lap. She was never nervous, never forgot what she wanted to say, nothing was out of order. That was Kate - always knew what she wanted.

Games and Songs

As much as Kate had a universal appreciation for people and nature, she had the same energy for games. She was a fierce competitor and approached each "game" with a great sense of adventure. She played everything from jacks to croquet with a spirit of fun and the desire to win, which she often did. Card games were a particular specialty, and she and Arthur played bridge every Wednesday night. Arthur studied the subject in his usual obsessive manner, but to Kate the game came naturally and she was the better player. She taught her grandchildren and young friends to play hearts and old maid, as well as some card games currently out of fashion such as fantan or smut (the loser has his nose anointed with ashes from the fireplace). All bets and antes were made with match sticks or, occasionally, pennies, if there were enough in the jar she kept on the sideboard.

Kate enjoyed the social aspect of bridge and the closeness of the less serious games, but she was a tough opponent and she loved winning. Always the teacher, she was glad to share the tricks of winning with anyone in any game. However she never lost on purpose or lied about what she held in her hand.

She was, of course, a wonderful storyteller. In the cool evening air, in the swings on the front porch, the family would gather to tell stories and sing songs. Kate knew many. Some she had learned from the former slaves on the plantations of her youth. She was able to do the shout and accompanying dance into her nineties. Some she'd learned from the mountain people of North Georgia and the Carolinas. A great surprise for me was when I opened a music book to learn a British folk song collected and arranged by Benjamin Britten, only to discover my grandmother had already taught me "Oliver Cromwell laid buried and dead," learned in her youth from the same Appalachians who had taught the song to Cecil Sharp and Benjamin Britten.

A family favorite elimination game was William Ma'Trembletoes, played like "One potato Two potato" or "Engine, Engine Number Nine." Everyone stands in a circle, fist your hands and hold them in front of you in the center.

William Ma'Trembletoes:

William Ma'Trembletoes was a good fisherman
Catches hens puts them in pens
Some lay eggs and some lay none
Wire ...wire Limberlock
Sets and sings at twelve o'clock.
Three cuckos in a nest
One flew east and one flew west and One flew
over the old crow's nest.
O-U-T spells out.

One hand goes out. Start again.

The Shout: This dance is done as a shuffle, half bent over. We know the hand motions from "hand-bone". This Shout is mostly unknown today. Notice the relationship between the singer and God.

Shout from South Georgia, near Albany. Begin by shouting 'oly man or 'oly woman.

> You better live 'umble
> You better live mild.
> You better live like-a dat heabenly chile.

> When I gets to heab'n I spects to stop,
> Choose my seat and den sit down,
> Argue wid de Father, chatter wid de Son,
> Talk about de worl' dat I jus' come from,
> Talk about the green tree die as well as de dry-a
> De green tree die jus' as well as de dry-a –

> O Lawdy!

> Walk steady chillun, study yo'selves-a
> Jus lemme tell you 'bout God Himself-a,
> When He was a-walkin' here below
> Betwixt de eart' and den de sky,somethin' like a
>   Jericho-a
> Eatin' of de honey and drinkin' of de wine...

> O Lawdy!

> Simon Cyrene gwine dig my grave,

Angel Gab'l gwine hol' me down,
Hol' me down with a golden chain –

O Lawdy!

Tallulah Reed Lyons is the second grandaughter. She and
her sister were the grand-children who lived closest to Kate and
Arthur in Ainsley Park, in fact right around the corner.

A Glimpse of our Grandmother

She was the essence of her ancestry
and bore the marks of aristocratic heritage.
She stepped forth with authority and grace,
and with poet's magic she transformed
 A hot dog lunch into a gourmet feast
with a junket dessert into a sumptuous sundae,
Mismatched "Woolworth's" cups turned to finest
      crystal,
crockery to Chinese porclin
And paper napkins into hand-loomed Irish-linen.

We had not been invited - summoned.
"We'll have a ladies' little luncheon party
out by Canebreak on Saturday.
Be there at noon."

We might have had other plans or no
desire to come -
but the summons was only to be honored.

She greeted us with place cards
cut from last year's Christmas greetings.
Her cotton house dress hung elegantly
as a silken gown.
Her size five shoes from the "Nearly New"
matched the stride of any society dame
and with pride she came,
And she transformed:
Peanut butter on Ritz Crackers into caviar hor
    d'oerves
canned fruit punch into golden champaign
and clumsy ill-at-ease children into sparkling
    conversationalists
All enjoying the grand delights
of a "ladies' little luncheon party."

Tallulah Reed Lyons for this work, 1978.

I like it that both guest-poets chose tea parties as her theme.
I have included one of Kate's poems in answer.

Afternoon Tea

You guests who stir your neighborly cheer
In the cups of my bubbling tea,
The Clock over there would be greeting you too,
And so would the Cloisonne, heron-blue,
That Grandmother gave to me.

For the Vase on the top of my mantle shelf,
Has swayed her sceptor of golden-rod,
Of crocus, or mistletoe,
And graced like a queen she has welcomed you

here
In her robings of sky and foam
To the kingly court of the ticking Clock,
And the ember lights of home.
To you friends who scatter your ripples of mirth
On the pools of my yellow tea,
Please speak to the Clock, who's a chatterbox too
And smile with the Cloisonne, hereon-blue,
That Grandmother gave to me.

unpublished 1950

The Poems

It is nearly impossible to choose just a few of Kate Codington's poems from her three small books of poetry. I have chosen those which I've felt are indicative of her style, but they are no means the only ones, or even the best ones. The following poems are from the books Shod With Light, April Thoughts, and Ark of the Everglades.

With Waters Fresh Returning

Keep me, O Father,
Safe in time of sleeping.
Not as lilies
Withered at darkness;
Not as owl-wings
Hiding from light.
Help me to wake
With dawn on dawn arising
From night on night.
And give my life
No reason for departure,
No exit for retreat.
But like a wheel
With waters fresh returning,
Oh, may it bring
New purpose to my hands,
New dances to my feet.

Rimmings Of Spring

You alone, bare rock,
dare to refuse
embellishment of spring.
You, a battleship,
plowing the sea
of oak and hickory;
tossing the waves in flippant elegance;
your prow
set to that far and frigid luminance
the Northern Star.

I come to you, gray stone,
as Moses came,
seeking an altar in the wilderness
on which to offer God
simplicity of praise.
I come and find
(rimming each granite chink)
green of emerald
moss lichens so minute
they scarce can hold my tears
falling suddenly
as tears of spring.

Late Summer

Not only flowers receive the sun
Down his long journey to autumn senescence.
But now at the time of the slaying petals
And winter begun,
My heart is reluctant to part with its treasure

Light without measure.
Not so the zinnia, a gaudy fluorescence —
Faded to rust,
Dropping her seeds with torpor of slumber
Into the dust,
And callous, though scarlet and gold shall
    rebloom
Over her tomb.

Giving To Wind And Star

I watch December boughs against the sky
Extend their silent patterns on the cold;
Creating form as branches inter-ply
Like balance fugue of voices manifold.
And I with them, reach forth in naked line
Myself, unmarred from April flowering,
And show the hidden shape of my design,
Devoid of green entanglements of spring.

With boughs I lift myself to heaven's wall
Stripped of pretense - a stark, a winter tree;
Giving to wind and star in knotty scroll
The structure of a soul's integrity.
Shameless I stand, whatever be my form
Symetrical, or broken from the storm.

Some Early Spring

I must be gone,
Nor heed your curse nor blessing.
Orion stalks the August of the skies
And Cygnus flutters in a net of stars.
I too must run the curvature of years
Another spark to swim the Milky Way
Or float the luminosity of heaven.
But I'll return A quickened star.
And light that was my eyes
Will merge the spring,
And touch the earth
With blue of hyacinths.

Snow Storm (Villanelle)

Though lost in snow my April thoughts remain.
All flower like the crystals wink and bloom;
And so I learn of happiness in pain.
Your voice, departed, echoes once again,
Irradiant as dawn across the gloom.

Though lost in snow my April thoughts remain
Can joy your dereliction thus explain?
Yet memories recapture and relume
And so I learn of happiness in pain.
The richness of your mind is my domain;
Each filigree and cobble I assume.

Though lost in snow my April thoughts remain
Let elegy of love be my refrain
And permanent as carvings on a tomb.

And so I learn of happiness in pain.
If cudgeled, still a harlequin will claim
His cap and bells; and witches ride a broom.
Though lost in snow my April thoughts remain
And so I learn of happiness in pain.

Reminiscent of Bach

The ivy presumes ten thousand years
In shaping her fugue to the chapel wall
And makes indelible the tone
Of her green music,
Resonant with stone.
New vine ascends, but only to repeat
The ancient theme,
The polyphonic form -
Star, star, and star, and still more leafy stars
Through cadence, clef and chord -
An also universe
Whose pattern is the Lord.

The Schubert Quartet

We fought with music –
we the four -
our bows like battle sabers,
seaying stabbing,
glassanding down to nothingness;
while interwove

with static of our faces – tense as frozen flowers,
worshiping abstraction
omnipotent as love.

When morning came
with gray and empty sky,
we sought again the oracle.
But eyes were drooped with apathy,
and notes and dotted spaces
vague as angel tracts.
And we forgot antiphonies of tone
can reunite like stars among the billows,
astonishing with light.

Cutting The Gardenia Blossoms

White moons ascending
The midnight green of leaves,
Sculptured roses,
Passionate fragrance,
Have you no cry Beneath my scissors –
Clipping, clipping
As one would clip the tresses of a god?
And now I ask a question,
Unsolved by heaven or earth–
What lust of mine is this
Which seeks completion in
your
young
death?

Bayou Nocturn

Too long the moon upon a white magnolia -
I close my window.
Darkness
But as rain upon the shutter
A rush of petals opening
In utter
fragrancy.
Too long the moon upon a white magnolia.
Too long Diana.
In silver tension
Withholds her arrow.
Before the dawn,
The hour of her retreating,
In pale surrender
I turn the key that bars her magic tremor,
Her sandal kiss,
And pagan vows repeating,
Lay bare my heart, a target for her splendor.

Fairy Tale

I tossed my heart upon the grass.
A tree sprung up the morning after -
Mulberry-green and apricot-gold -
Shaken with laughter.

I stood quite vacant like a horn,
His music fled.
But knew relief
A mother knows when her child is born;
A culprit knows when truth is told;
Or mercy stems from grief.

The Ballad of Briar Rose

What matter brambles sharp as steel,
(Filling the mote, climbing the tower)
For I, a prince of gay romance,
Shall break the magic power...
The spines divide. I enter, pass
The king, the queen, the snoring groom,
The cook who slapped the stable boy,
The fool, his legs about a broom.
On, on they sleep, or so pretend.
Who knows, perhaps they fake a nap?
(To seize my gold the royal pair has laid a trap.)
So What? I laugh and climb the stair
And wander hall and room galore.
Then far upon a dizzy height,
Behold a door!
And here I find you, beautious one.
In mists of spider web you lie.
But on your lips, and through your curls
The sunlight twinkles roguishly.

I give my kiss. Nor shall I fear
The startled court, the blasting horn,
If in your heart, O briar Rose,
I find no other thorn.

Beauty Speaks To The Beast
(Fairy Tale)

Your eyes are pits of fire,
Your jaw, a lions jaw.
Savagery and hate perhaps
Are prisoned in your paw.

And yet no soldier guards the palace gate,
No cannon dares attack -
Roses, roses climb the colonnades
And spread their tents in still of bivouac.

Can there be cruelty in red of roses,
Or avarice by gold corollas blown?
Or hate in petals, white and moon-emotional
As of this blossom, pledged to me alone?

What though my Father fret, and Sister grieve?
Fearless, I stay, and fearlessly believe
That you who rule with flowers
Tear no flesh apart.
Nor will you shred the purity
Of roses in my heart.

Gloria In Excelsis

All was dark
And then a glimmer winked,
Straddled a ray of dust
And suddenly
Shook a yellow flower in her face.
And though the time was August

And indolence of days,
The girl - long blinded and long ill,
Sensing a newness and a magnitude,
Reached forth her arms, and so
Made tangible her praise.

Victorian Love

Into the morning
We rode our horses.
The wind laughed
And the sun
Tinkled his golden bells.
Straight we sat in splendor,
Held by Victorian check-reins
Curbing the prancing bays.

No one spoke.
But eyes sparked,
Lips trembled, and our love -
Tuned to the galloping hoofs,
Floated - a white scarf behind us.

Oh, was this love
Or but enchantment,
That dared not kiss nor clasp;
Yet with a young delirium,
Embroidered tales of princess
And of knight,
The while
Overwhelming us with roses.
But the touch of your hand
Stung with the burn
And beauty of a bee.

Irresolute I Stood Beside The River

Irresolute, I stood beside the river.
Had I been reckless in my predilection
I might have drowned beneath the whirling water.

But timidly I felt along the border,
And stealthily I steeled my soul for action.
While rushes kissed and broke in opal bubbles;
And reeds, relenting, bowed a meek surrender.
In reverence I weighed the ancient question
Of human cowardice and human courage,
Of human frailty and human power.
And so I reached my arms. I prayed, I struggled,
And clutched my fear as though it were a dagger,
And flung it far into the burning heaven.

And like a willow bough a-float. at random,
Or birchen bark of racing light and silver,
With joy and praise I swam the mighty river.

Apple Orchard

No youth however nimble can attain
Blossoming boughs.
Only the old through retrospect explain
Orchards of bloom - visions that rouse
White heaven in minds too atrophied to heed
Wisdom of fallen fruit and bitter seed.

Old Age

Go look in a well
When the moon is high,
Till ripples rise
Up to your eyes;
Till coping the rim
Coil and swim
With frothing of gold
Red gold of the earth-heart.
Go look to remember,
Then look to forget
The silver jet
(Sweet and awry)
Of a chill
Rill
Where buttercups flash
And chickadees dart,
And joy is a cradle-song
Rocking the hill.

At Noon There Is No Shadow

At noon there is no shadow.
Now a tree contracts unto itself,
And uncontrolled
By trailing gray and violet madder
Blazes with emerald.

And even I, at moments may become
The center of creation
And a will
Released from vaguery

And drift of shade
I drink the burning vigor of the gods
Myself a god
And to the sun a brother.
At noon there is no shadow.

He Too Was Young

It happened at the funeral of a girl -
Her casket weighted by a load of bloom
White lilies patterned flat in crowns of pearl.
The preacher said, "For her no death, no doom.
"Absolved of sin, to heaven I pass her soul,
"Rejoiced to go. For life is rigorous, sad,
"Accurst through Adam's fall. Today she's whole,

"Washed in the Savior's blood. And she is glad."

At this the lilies raised their pallid heads.
And shook their petals madly to the floor;
The coffin opened wide;
The startled sun retreated from the door.
The maiden spoke, "In all of this you lie.
"Christ too was young. Did he not hate to die?"

A Rainbow Lingered

A rainbow lingered on the hill,
More flower-like than flowers –
Rose and blue and cardinal
Between the summer showers.

And these you followed though your eyes
Were blinded by the rain
Orange, red and violet
And hues that intervene.
Against the bluster of the storm
Your unrelenting will
Refracted skies to indigo,
Vermillion, daffodil.

Earth colors arched the years for you
In tones of mist and sun
Crimson, gold and lavender
Till darkness made them one.

Color Prints

I

A poplar stands beside the door.
(But those I love are grown and gone)
October smites the leaves with gold
And shelters me with a roof of stars.
0 sons return before the snow,
The sleet –
And broken bough.

II

Wisteria climbs the trellises –
Twine on twine of stem and mist.
Now
Morning shakes the vine with light
And I am lost in blossoming.
O spring remain,
Lest winter blind.
My eyes to amethyst.

To Autumn

Hold me,
O Autumn,
Dialed to this hour
Of crimson oak and aster flower,
Nor let me cower
To winter mockery, and, cold
Intrepid peace I cannot yet desire.

Hold me, bright days,
And brand me with your fire;
That God may see, nor trust me soon to go
With crumpled leaf, and flurry of the snow.

Advent In the Woods

I walked the woods
Where knotted trees

Like charcoal sketches
Sprawled the sky —
All separate,
Yet interwove
As old philosophy.

I walked the woods,
When suddenly
Dejection ceased
Its harrowing
Bright from the manger
A blue-gray violet
Announced the spring.

The Song of Diana

Shod with light I run the skies -
Spiral and nebula shoal upon shoal -
Urging my hounds to the uttermost goal
Stars of the Milky Way sparkle and glow -
Ashes and fire and blossoms of snow.

When moons and their planets have darkened to
    one
And thong of my sandal is broken or shred,
My hunger may yearn for a human home,
My weariness cry for a human bed.
But love of a goddess is sharper than flame;
And young lips tremble to speak my name.

So feet of Diana are never at rest;

And her arrows in heaven are swift as the rain.
"Hi, yi, and to heel! Off dogs and away"
Though the gods are forgot and the antelope
    slain...
Hi, Yi! For perhaps on that nethermost shore
Wisdom is waiting and sleeps no more.

Notes

April Thoughts : A Collection of Poems by Kate Fort Codington

Shod With Light : A Collection of Poems by Kate Fort Codington

Other Poems

Blue Ridge Mountain Pictures, 1940, *54*
A Legend of Nacoochee, J. Fischer Bros. New York, NY.,
1916, *39*
Lollipop, 1920, *65*
Woman to Man, 1916, *157*

Included Short Stories – These short stories are undated,
although I have guessed their dates from their content. There is
no record of them ever having been published, although they
may have been.

Above The Storm, *115*
Abraham, Issac and Jacob, *83*
The Big Family, *74*
Bones of the Barracuda, *124*
Children of the Blue Ridge (A Narrative of the American
Caste), *42*
Dog House, *145*
The Frog Pond, *88*
The Other David, *56*

Poems and Reminiscences of Others

Zests of Earth. *Pure Fragrancies & Mortal Vagrancies*, A
Collection of Poems by Arthur Codington, 1966, *64*
Why Our Capital Grows. *Jest About Georgia : A Limerick
Cycle by Arthur Codington*, Longino and Porter, Atlanta,
1952, *144.*

A Glimpse of Our Grandmother, Tallulah Reed Lyons, 1979, *166.*
Portrait of a Lady, Aurelia Austin, 1975, *12.*
William Ma'Trembletoes, Traditional children's game, *164.*
A Southern Shout. Traditional folk song, South Georgia, *144.*

Sources:

Codington, John Fort. Personal communication, 1975.

Codington, Kate Fort. *April Thoughts.* The Deynor Press, Mamarameck, NY., 1966.

Codington, Kate Fort, *The Ark of the Everglades.* The Print Shop, Atlanta, Ga.,1975.

Codington, Kate Fort, *Cypress Knees.* unpublished manuscript, n.d.

Codington, Kate Fort, *A Legend of Nacoochee,* J. Fischer & Bros., A Division of Belwin Mills Publishing Corp., 1916, New York, NY.

Codington, Kate Fort, *Shod With Light.* The Deynor Press, Mamaraneck, NY., 1966.

Coulter, E. Merton, *Georgia: A Short History.* The University of North Carolina Press, Chapel Hill, NC., 1947.

The Forts of Mt. Airy, Tri-County Advertiser, Centennial

Edition : 1879 - 1979. By the editors, Clarksville, Ga. 1979 p. 16.

Fort, Kate Haynes, *Memoirs of the Fort and Fannin Families*. Press of Macgowan & Cooke Co., Chattanooga, TN. 1903.

Fort, John Porter, *Memoirs of John Porter Fort*, transcribed and edited. by Martha Fort Anderson. Knickerbocker Press, New York, 1918.

Fort, John Porter, *The Story of an Apple*. Cornelia Enterprise Print, Cornelia, GA.

John Fort II, *Lets Talk About. Published* by the weekly newspaper The Northeast.

Fort, William Ellis, *"A Reminiscence: Christmas 1886."* 1975.

Hightower, Emily Anderson, Personal interview, Atlanta, GA. Sept. 1979.

Vivian Yeiser Laramour, "Miami Muse", *Miami Daily News*. Miami, FL. November 13, 1932.

Lewis, Ann E., ed., *First 500 Poems of Georgia Magazine*. Georgia Magazine, Atlanta, Ga. 1964.

McGail, H.L., The Adjutant General, personal letter to the Commissioner of Pensions, State of Georgia, Atlanta, Georgia, June 14, 1915, Dept, of Archives and History, Atlanta, GA.

Milz, Barbara, "Court Official Retiring - But He Won't Be Idle," Atlanta Journal-Constitution. Atlanta, GA., 1956.

Norris, Jack C., *Dr. Tomlinson Fort, A Discussion of the Man and His Historic Book : A Treatise On Internal Medicine-1849.* Atlanta, GA. 1970.

Northern, William F., Ed., *Men of Mark in Georgia*, vol II, A.B. Caldwell Co., Atlanta GA, 1906.

Redfearn, Susan Fort, *Lulah Ellis Fort*, 1935.

Shafer, Catherine Codington, Personal interview, South Miami, FL., Sept. 1979.

Shafer, Catherine Codington, Personal letter, 1981.

About the author:

Former Park Guide on the Freedom Trail for Boston National Historical Park, archivist and history teacher, Dory Codington is better known for her historical adventures than for literary analysis. She blogs history and romance at http://DorysHistoricals.com, and her novels in the Edge of Empire Series, about Colonial, Revolutionary and Provincial history, can be found at the usual online booksellers, and local bookstores throughout the Boston, Massachusetts area. Dory received her BA and MA in American history from Wellesley College and Brandeis University. She has a MLIS in archival science from Simmons College. She lives in Massachusetts with a husband, a daughter, a son and a tortoise.

Dory's other books are adventure romance novels based on and in the era of the American Revolution. They are::

Cardinal Points
Fate and Fair Winds
Beside Turning Water

The cover for this book was designed by Daniel M. Silverstein.

The cover photo was taken by Kate's neighbor and friend by Devereaux McClatchy, probably in 1970.

The work was carefully copy-edited by Mark L. Silverstein, for which I am profoundly grateful.

The book layout and design are by me, as are all mistakes, mislabeling of photographs, and inaccuracies.